YORK HANDBOOKS

GENERAL EDITOR:
Professor A.N. Jeffares
(*University of Stirling*)

ENGLISH USAGE

Colin G. Hey
MA (WALES) MA ED (BIRMINGHAM)

 LONGMAN
YORK PRESS

YORK PRESS
Immeuble Esseily, Place Riad Solh, Beirut.

LONGMAN GROUP LIMITED
Longman House,
Burnt Mill,
Harlow,
Essex.

© Librairie du Liban 1984

First published 1984
ISBN 0 582 79268 1
Printed in Hong Kong by
Sheck Wah Tong Printing Press Ltd

Contents

Part 1

The English language

The evolution of the English language

All students of English should know, at least in outline, how the language originated and developed. It is a fascinating story and the tale is still far from complete as the language is growing and changing all the time: usage changes, words are borrowed from foreign languages and new words are coined. Britain's imperial past, bringing its people into intimate contact with a wide variety of races and languages in almost every part of the globe, accounts for thousands of words being incorporated into the language, and the influence of immigration over the centuries has been another powerful factor. A consequence of Britain's imperial and colonial past is that English is spoken by hundreds of millions all over the world – in America, Canada, Australia, Asia and Africa – and it has become the world's leading international language.

Origins

English belongs to the Teutonic or Germanic branch of the Indo-European family of languages. The term 'English' was originally used to denote the language spoken by the Anglo-Saxon and Frisian tribes who settled in some strength in the North East of England in the fifth and sixth centuries.

We can point to three main stages of development: (1) Old English (sometimes known as 'Anglo-Saxon') up to 1100, (2) Middle English from 1100 to 1500, and (3) Modern English. The development of the language was, of course, gradual, without clear-cut divisions. The Middle English period was greatly influenced by the Norman Conquest of 1066 and during the latter part of this period the influences of Wyclif's (1324–84) translation of the Bible into English (1380) and the poetry of Geoffrey Chaucer (1340–1400), author of *The Canterbury Tales*, helped to establish the beginnings of Modern English.

The modern period was further signalled by the introduction into England of printing by William Caxton (1421–91) and by the Renaissance (the Revival of Classical Learning). The Revival of Learning brought with it an enthusiasm for the study of Latin and Greek, and many words were introduced into our language in consequence. Scholars for a time tended to look down on the boorishness and inelegance of English, but a counter-influence soon made itself felt when the break with Rome occurred and the Protestant religion was established in England during the period of the Reformation in the sixteenth century. The Bible as well as prescribed forms of church service were printed in English, and became widely available.

The Angles, Saxons and Jutes

Before the coming of the Germanic tribes, Britain had been under the domination of the Romans since 55BC. The original natives of our island were Celtic. Many resisted the Romans and fled westwards into what is now known as Wales and Cornwall, but the remainder lived alongside the Romans, acquired some skill in the colloquial Latin language of the day and absorbed their conquerors' customs. It was when the Romans withdrew around the fourth century that the Germanic tribes began to invade Britain and establish the language that developed into English.

Today about five-sixths of our everyday vocabulary consists of words of Germanic origin. The majority of these are associated first with ordinary domestic and family matters, with food, clothing, the home, furniture, tools and implements, for example *mother, child, bread, cloth, hearth, kettle, plough*. Next we have the names of common objects in nature: the heavenly bodies, trees, plants, animals, the seasons of the year, the weather, parts of the body and emotions, for example *sun, field, oak, grass, horse, fire, rain, Spring, day, month, foot, neck, mouth, sweat, sit, run, love, hate*. Most of our pronouns, numerals, prepositions, conjunctions, many adverbs of time and place, the auxiliary verbs and most single-syllable verbs and nouns also belong to the period.

The Vikings

With the coming of Christianity from AD596 onwards a considerable number of Latin words, many borrowed originally from Greek and mostly associated with religion, came into the language. Then followed yet another invasion, that of the Scandinavian Vikings towards the end of the eighth century. They ravaged the eastern and northeastern coasts and eventually established themselves in the kingdoms of Northumbria, East Anglia and Mercia. Their language was closely related to the established Old English.

The Norman Conquest

In 1066 yet another invasion of great significance occurred – the Norman Conquest. A steady stream of Norman–French dialect words began to flow into our language. These words were derived from words of Latin origin and were to be found throughout Europe in the colloquial language of daily life. It was from the common core of Latin that the related groups of Romance (that is, Roman-based) languages evolved – Italian, Spanish, French, Portuguese.

By 1350 the native English language had been saturated by the all-pervading influence of Norman–French and on top of this the vocabulary of the separately developed Parisian French found daily currency in the language of the Norman nobility, in the church and the learned professions. This led to the emergence of a language of style and flexibility capable of elegant literary expression.

Standard English

With the passage of time, distinct English dialects emerged and developed in different parts of Britain. Gradually the East Midland or Mercian dialect, now referred to as the Southern dialect, came to be accepted as the most important as it was the language of London, of the Court and of Oxford and Cambridge. So it came to be the pattern of standard English. Its prestige was further enhanced, as we have seen, by being the language of Wyclif's Bible and by the writings of Geoffrey Chaucer; and the coming of printing did much to consolidate the Southern dialect in its pre-eminent status.

Chaucer gave English forms to many French words and helped to set the mould for what we refer to as Modern English. His influence was incalculable and he is rightly called 'the father of the English language'.

The weakening of inflexion

Throughout the evolution of modern English one striking characteristic has been the gradual weakening of inflexion. Inflexions are those changes in the form of words to show differences in grammatical relationship and differences in meaning: *he, him, his; cat, cats; sing, sings, sang, sung; great, greater*. From being originally a highly inflected language, like Latin or Arabic, Modern English has eliminated the greater proportion of these inflexions. Flexibility and subtlety of expression is now achieved by the increased use of prepositions – *of, to, for* and *by* (instead of using difference in 'case') – and still more in the use of the auxiliary verbs, such as *be, have, do, shall, will, may*. Gender in the noun, in the sense we find it in French, where *table* is feminine and *wall* masculine, disappeared and was replaced by distinctions based on sex and animateness in which *boy* is masculine, *girl* feminine and *tables* and *walls* neuter.

Vocabulary expansion

The successive invasions of Britain followed by the coming of the Renaissance resulted in a dramatic expansion of the vocabulary of English. By the sixteenth century many thousands of words of various origins had been incorporated into Modern English. During the centuries that followed, mainly because of the greater intermingling of peoples throughout the world, the vocabulary continued to expand. In this development we can point to three particular categories:

(1) Foreign words borrowed in a close approximation to their original form. Examples:

Word	Origin	Word	Origin
anorak	Eskimo	cognac	French
apartheid	Afrikaans	divan	Persian/Arabic
arpeggio	Italian	dungarees	Hindi
ballerina	Italian	fiancé	French
banana	West African	galore	Irish
boomerang	Aboriginal	ghetto	Italian
	(Australia)	gourmand	French
café	French	guerrilla	Spanish
cafeteria	Spanish	mayonnaise	French
canoe	Spanish (Haiti)	restaurant	French
cliché	French	snorkel	German

(2) Foreign words that have been anglicised in form and/or meaning. Examples:

Word	Origin	Word	Origin
algebra	Arabic	dragoon	French
almanac	Arabic	gambit	Italian
assassin	Arabic	judo	Japanese
bayonet	French	tattoo	Polynesian
chutney	Hindi	thug	Hindi
curfew	French	yoghurt	Turkish

(3) Newly coined words (neologisms) mostly concerned with science, technology, new products, discoveries and inventions. These are usually formed from Latin or Greek roots. Examples:

acronym	embolism	penicillin	schizophrenia
aneurism	gerontology	paediatrics	telescope
audiometer	hyperthermia	psychology	television
automobile	hypodermic	psychosomatic	thermometer
biochemistry	optometrist	quasar	troposphere

Some neologisms have become very familiar but others are not so well known: see 'Nouns of assembly', p. 78, and 'Phils, phobias, ologies and isms', p. 79.

Alongside these clear-cut borrowings and coinages, we must not forget the earlier phenomenon, largely the result of the Renaissance in and after the sixteenth century, when the practice developed of forming new English words with the aid of classical prefixes and suffixes. This resulted in the formation of thousands of words such as:

reconstruction, ineligible, illusion, irrevocable, intermission, substantially, ineradicable, invisible, disseminate, supercilious, exculpate, precedent, subjugate, persuade, torture, coherent

In spite of all these inroads into English, most of everyday English vocabulary still consists of words of Germanic origin. These are the words still closest to the joys and sorrows of life and for this reason they play a major role in certain types of prose and in drama and poetry when feelings and emotions predominate.

Part 2

Clearing the ground

BEFORE ESTABLISHING a flower or vegetable garden, a good gardener cultivates his plot. He clears out persistent weeds and then prepares the soil to receive the cuttings or seeds which, in due course, will develop into strong, healthy plants. Similar care must be taken by students of the English Language. First of all we must get rid of the 'weeds' that are detrimental to the healthy growth of language. We can do this by learning to recognise common mistakes in grammar, usage and style. We must then proceed to the acquisition of good language habits.

Without entering into arguments about the concept of 'correctness' in language, we can reasonably claim that custom and good manners demand the acceptance of certain standards of English usage. Our aim, therefore, is to help young writers to avoid words, expressions and constructions that may strike an educated reader as being either lacking in taste or as being plainly wrong. Often we can declare categorically that a word or expression is wrong in a particular context, but occasionally the comments 'acceptable', 'unacceptable' or 'inappropriate' would be nearer the truth. Throughout this book we have in mind the requirements of examinations in English – at home and abroad – where traditional usage and conservative practice are still demanded.

1. Adverbs
When writing be sure to use the correct adverb form to modify a verb:

Right He speaks very loudly. (*Wrong* loud)
Right The car stopped quite suddenly. (*Wrong* sudden)

Note that in casual speech some frequently occurring adjectives like 'slow', 'quick' are used as adverbs, as in 'Come quick' and 'You're walking too slow.'

2. Agreement
Students should be aware of three types of agreement in English:

(*a*) When the present tense is used, a singular subject must be followed by a singular verb:

Right This baby cries all the time.
Right These babies cry all the time.

(b) When parts of 'to be' are used, the verb must agree with the number of its subject:

Right   Every one of the boys was at the meeting.
Right   All the girls were going to the university.
Right   The bank manager and his staff are very helpful.
Wrong Neither of the boxers were very skilful.

(c) Possessive adjectives must agree with the nouns they refer back to:

Right   Each boy gave his report.
Right   The girl showed her ticket to the inspector.
Right   The children carried their books home from school.

Collective nouns like 'committee', 'department', 'government' sometimes present difficulties. It is best to treat such a word as plural when the emphasis is on the various members, but as singular when the whole body is being considered. For example:

A committee *was* set up to discuss the problem. (A body was set up.)
The committee *were* in disagreement on some points.
(Here we have in mind the individuals concerned.)

A more serious error would be to change from singular to plural (or from plural to singular) in the same sentence, as in this example:

The firm *has* made remarkable progress during the year and *have* increased their sales considerably.

Note that an apparently plural subject may have a singular verb if the subject is being considered as a single entity. For example:

Twelve months *is* a long time to wait.
The United Nations *has* decided ...

3. all right, all ready, already, all together, altogether

Note the different usages carefully:

Within two days of the accident I felt *all right* again. (Note that there is no such word as *alright*; never use it.)

The travellers were *all ready* by dawn.
By that time I had *already* heard the news.

The first party set off in twos and threes; the second group started off *all together*.
Altogether there were twenty boys in the class.

4. allusion, illusion

An allusion is an indirect or incomplete reference:

The speaker made an allusion to the problems they had overcome.
The poem contained many classical allusions.

An illusion is a deceptive appearance:

The art of the conjuror depends largely on optical illusions.

I have often seen the illusion of pools of water in the desert.

5. because

Wrong   The reason he is late is because he missed the train.

Wrong   Why he won the prize was because he had worked very steadily.

Right   He was late because he had missed the train.

Right   He won the prize because he had worked very steadily.

If you use 'because' you do not need to duplicate the idea with the words 'reason' and 'why'.

Similarly it is wrong to write:

The *cause* of the bankruptcy was *due to* poor sales.

Here the word 'cause' is a duplication of the idea of 'due to'. The correct version is: 'The cause of the bankruptcy was poor sales.'

6. beside, besides

Beside means 'next to'; *besides* means 'in addition to'.

Right   The speaker was sitting beside the chairman.

Right   There were three people on the platform besides the speaker.

7. can, may

Can expresses ability to do something; *may* expresses permission or the possibility of doing something.

Right   May I be excused lectures on Saturday morning, please?

Right   I can obtain copies of the lectures from my friends.

Wrong   Can I borrow your pen, please?

Note that *might* and *could* are the past tense forms of *may* and *can*:

He wondered if he might be excused lectures on Saturday.

8. Case

Case only applies to six words in the English language. This means that these words have different forms when they are used as subjects and objects. The words concerned are I/me, he/him, she/her, we/us, they/them and who/whom. The following examples show how these pronouns work:

Right   I like him but he doesn't like me.

Right   We can't visit her tonight but she will try to visit us soon.

Right   Those are the men who visited France.

Right   This is Mr Smith whom we met last year.
Right   Give it to me, not to him.
Right   The bank manager asked my wife and me to call to see him.
Wrong The bank manager asked my wife and I to call to see him.
Right   There is no disagreement between him and me.
Wrong There is no disagreement between him and I.
Right   It is right for us older boys to set a good example.
Wrong It is right for we older boys to set a good example.

9. chronic

This word is frequently used incorrectly. It means 'of long duration', not 'severe' or 'acute'.

Right   He suffers from chronic indigestion. (the trouble is long standing)
Wrong The football team gave a chronic performance. (very bad performance)

10. Clichés

This is a French word, now completely incorporated into English. It means words or phrases that have been so frequently used that they have lost their freshness: they have become hackneyed. A cliché is like a well-worn coin whose sharp definition has been lost for ever. Clichés are to be avoided in precise writing, though they may be more easily tolerated in casual speech. The following are commonly used clichés:

explore every avenue; leave no stone unturned; too funny for words; conspicuous by his absence; at this moment in time

11. compare with, compare to

In a comparison where the emphasis is on possible differences, the correct usage is 'compared with'; but where resemblances are suggested the construction is 'compared to'. Here are examples:

Right   *Compared with* the French, we British have less imagination in the art of cooking.
Right   Witnesses *compared* the sound of the explosion *to* a tremendous thunder-clap.

12. compare, contrast

To compare is to put side by side things that resemble each other. To contrast is to put side by side things that clearly differ. For example:

You cannot compare the quality of picture on colour television with that of black and white.

The flatness of Sudan contrasts dramatically with the mountainous terrain of neighbouring Ethiopia.

13. contrary
The two phrases 'on the contrary' and 'to the contrary' should be distinguished. The first implies a contradiction and normally occurs at the beginning of a sentence:

On the contrary, I do not know him. Indeed I have never met him.

'To the contrary' tends to follow 'nothing':

I have heard nothing to the contrary and so I assume he will come.

14. continual, continuous
Continual describes actions (often annoying) which recur frequently. *Continuous* describes actions which do not stop.

Right   How can you put up with these continual interruptions?
Right   There was continuous bombing from 8 a.m. until noon.

15. council, counsel
Council is the term given to a committee or administrative body. A person who serves on a town council is called a 'councillor'.

Counsel means advice or opinion offered. In law, 'counsel' is a practising barrister who sometimes gives legal counsel. The transitive verb 'to counsel' means 'to give advice'.

16. Dangling or hanging participles
These terms refer to the very common fault of not relating a participle to its proper noun or pronoun. Study the following sentences carefully:

Wrong   *Coming* down the hill into the town, the fishing boats could be seen in the harbour busily unloading their catches.
Right   *Coming* down the hill into the town, *we* could see the fishing boats in the harbour busily unloading their catches.

In the second sentence the present participle has a subject 'we'.

Wrong   *Watching* the documentary film, the problems of the unemployed were obvious to everybody.
Right   *Watching* the documentary film, *the audience* could clearly see the problems of the unemployed.

Here the participle 'watching' has 'the audience' as subject.

Wrong   *Having finished* all my letters, they were posted immediately.
Right   *Having finished* all my letters, *I* posted them immediately.

H. W. Fowler in his book *Modern English Usage* is prepared to make a few concessions, for he is willing to accept 'Roughly speaking, what you say is true.' This is equivalent to 'What you say is approximately true.'

Some borderline examples are worth noting: many business letters might read: 'Referring to your letter, you state that you found the goods damaged when they reached you.' Even though the meaning is clear it would be sensible in an English examination to write:

> *Referring* to your letter, *I note* that you claim that the goods were damaged when they reached you.

17. Defining and non-defining clauses

These are terms applied to relative clauses. The clauses may look alike but they perform different functions in a sentence. The following examples illustrate the differences:

> The news that arrived at noon was very optimistic.

This is a defining clause, completing the information about the news. Such defining clauses are introduced by the relative pronouns 'that', 'who' and 'which':

> The book *that* I bought . . .
> The woman *who* came in . . .
> The bird *which* sings . . .

A non-defining or commenting clause adds some additional information to the subject as in the following example:

> The news, which was quite unexpected, told us about the disaster.

Such commenting clauses are introduced by the same relative pronouns and are contained between commas; they could almost be written in brackets as a parenthesis as far as meaning is concerned.

> The discovery of the plot (which was soon to stun the country) was kept a secret for at least a week.

Here are two further examples:

> The strip of sea *that separates Britain from the continent* is called the English channel.   (This is a defining clause)

> The English channel, *which separates Britain from the continent*, is quite narrow.   (This is a non-defining or commenting clause.)

18. desert, dessert

These two words are frequently confused. Note carefully their meanings and how they are used:

> The Sahara *desert* is a vast and hostile area. (Note the stress – désert.)

> He would not *desert* his friends. (Here the stress is desért.)

The word 'dessert' is quite different, as the example shows:

> At their evening meal they had oranges, bananas and grapes for *dessert*.

This means a fruit or pudding course at a meal. The stress is on the second syllable – dessért.

19. different from, different to, different than

All the authorities seem to agree that it is wrong to imagine that 'different from' is the only correct usage, but in general we are warned to be wary of saying 'different to'.

Note the following carefully:

Right   English is *different from* German in that the latter is a highly inflected language.

Acceptable My feelings on my return home were very *different to* those I experienced at my departure.

United States usage prefers 'different than'.

20. Direct and indirect speech

Note carefully the differences between direct and indirect (or reported) speech, particularly in the use of commas:

Direct:
'Look here,' said the policeman, 'you can't leave your car parked in front of the shop.'
'Why did you pick on me?' demanded the angry driver.

Indirect:
The policeman told the driver that he could not leave his car in front of the shop. In reply the angry driver wanted to know why the policeman had picked on him.

In changing from direct to indirect speech present tenses are altered to past tenses, and pronouns in the first and second person move to the third person; adverbs of time move back in time, as in the following example:

Direct:
'I know you are feeling upset now,' said John to his friend Peter.

Indirect:
John said that he knew his friend Peter was feeling upset at that moment.

21. due to

Grammatically speaking, the authorities say that 'due to' is adjectival in function and should therefore, like a participle, be associated with a noun, as in these examples:

Fires due to carelessness cost millions of pounds,
The fire was due to carelessness.
His success was due to hard work.
The closing of the bank was due to threats of disorder.
(Here *closing* is a verbal noun)

The correct usage can be expressed in two rules:

(1) 'due to' can be a predicate relating to a particular noun, as in:
The discovery was due to Tom's keen observation.

(2) 'due to' can modify an antecedent noun, as in:
Strikes due to verbal misunderstandings are quite common.

It is generally considered incorrect to use 'due to' to introduce an adverbial phrase as in these examples:

Wrong Due to the rain the tennis championships were postponed.
Wrong The road accident occurred due to bad fog.

Students should be warned that examiners are inclined to deduct marks when 'due to' is wrongly used. The construction is not easy to understand, so students who feel uncertain should try to avoid the construction altogether. In its place they could use the construction 'owing to', or rephrase the sentence completely, as follows:

The heavy rain caused the tennis championships to be postponed.
Owing to the heavy rain the tennis championships were postponed.

22. effect, affect

These words are often confused. The simplest solution for a student is to use the former as a noun, meaning 'result' or 'change':

The effect of the new policy was immediately obvious.

and the latter as a verb meaning 'cause a change in':

The accusations against him did not affect our friendship.

23. except, accept

The word *except* is now mostly used as a preposition meaning 'not including':

Everyone except John will have to pay for the damage.

Accept is a verb meaning 'take' or 'receive':

I shall accept their invitation to visit their home.

24. fewer, less

Use *fewer* with numbers and before plural nouns:

Fewer than fifty people were present.
There are *fewer* trains in England now than there used to be.

Use *less* with uncountable nouns like 'rain', 'sunshine', 'money', 'bread', 'pleasure':

There was *less* rain than usual last month.
We have received *less* bread today so we shall be able to feed fewer children.

25. finally, at last

Finally can be used in two ways. It can be the equivalent of 'eventually':

After hours on the road, we finally reached Rome.

It can also introduce the last item in a series:

We must make a list of everything we are taking with us. We must then see that we have left nothing important behind. We must leave everything tidy and *finally* we must check that we have closed all the windows and doors.

At last suggests the end of a long wait:

At last, he could see the result of his efforts.
Thank goodness! The waiter is bringing our food at last.

It can also be used as an exclamation:

At last! We thought you were never going to get here!

26. get

Be careful how you use *get*. It is one of the most useful and therefore one of the most over-used verbs in the language. Though acceptable in many contexts in conversational English, it should be used sparingly in writing. The following advice may prove useful:

(*a*) It is inadvisable in writing to use the phrase 'have got' when you mean 'have' or 'possess'.

Avoid We've got a pony.
Better We've a pony.

Avoid We got there at 3 o'clock.
Better We arrived at 3 o'clock.

Avoid Will he get a prize?
Better Will he win a prize?

Avoid You've got to win this afternoon.
Better You must win this afternoon.

Avoid I'll get some milk from the refrigerator.
Better I'll fetch some milk from the refrigerator.

(*b*) The following idioms are acceptable in colloquial English:

That man gets on my nerves.   Get a move on.

(*c*) In American English the past participle *gotten* meaning 'acquired' is still in general use. The expression 'I've gotten me a new cabin-cruiser' is used to mean 'I've bought a new cabin-cruiser.'

The form *got* is often used colloquially by Americans, as in Britain, simply to mean 'have', as in 'I've got a bad cold.'

27. hardly, scarcely, no sooner

Hardly and *scarcely* are often followed by clauses beginning with 'when':

I had hardly opened the door *when* I was rudely interrupted.
The play had scarcely begun *when* the lights failed.

Notice that when *hardly* and *scarcely* occur at the beginning of a sentence there is inversion of the subject and predicate:

Hardly had I opened the door when I was rudely interrupted.
Scarcely had the play begun when the lights failed.

No sooner, on the other hand, is followed by a clause beginning with 'than':

I had no sooner knocked on the door *than* it was opened by a complete stranger.

Inversion can also occur with 'no sooner':

No sooner had I knocked on the door than it was opened by a complete stranger.

28. Hyphens

The correct use of hyphens presents many problems. Here are some guidelines:

(*a*) Established compounds like 'headmaster', 'bookcase', 'wallpaper', and 'today' need no hyphens.

(*b*) A hyphen is often used in compound adjectives when they precede a noun:

He was a well-dressed man.
Mr Roberts was always well dressed.
The Home-Rule Bill was easily defeated.
A Bill for Home Rule was presented to Parliament.

(*c*) Hyphens are usually required in compounds involving 'anti', 'ex', 'non' and 'vice', for example, *anti-aircraft, ex-serviceman, non-violence* and *vice-captain*.

(*d*) Hyphens should be used in words like *co-education, co-operation* and *re-emphasise*, where the co-occurrence of two vowels can cause difficulties of recognition and pronunciation.

29. imminent, eminent

These quite common words are often confused; both are adjectives. *Imminent* means 'likely to happen soon'; *eminent* means 'distinguished' or 'notable'.

According to the weathermen heavy storms are *imminent*.
He is an *eminent* physicist, a winner of a Nobel Prize.

30. imply, infer
These words have quite distinct meanings and cannot be used interchangeably. *Imply* means 'to suggest or hint'; *infer* means 'to deduce or draw a conclusion from a statement'. Look carefully at the following examples:

In my letter I *implied* that we were short of food, although I did not say so bluntly.
From my letter the officer in charge was bound to *infer* that our supplies were running short.

31. interested, disinterested, uninterested
These words are often wrongly used. *Disinterested* means 'indifferent', 'unbiased', 'not influenced by self-interest'. *Uninterested* simply means 'not interested in'; this is the negative form of 'interested'.

Right   My friend is *uninterested* in detective stories.
Wrong   He is quite *disinterested* in football; he hates the game.
Right   John was a *disinterested* party; he was quite outside the
           controversy and could give an unbiased opinion.

32. it is, it's, its
Many students have considerable difficulty with these words. Study the examples carefully if you are at all uncertain.

It is Saturday tomorrow.
It's cold today.   (the apostrophe indicates the missing 'i')
The dog chased *its* tail.   ('its' is the possessive adjective)

33. lay, lie
These verbs frequently cause problems. Study the various parts of the verbs carefully and then look at the examples.

TO LAY: transitive verb meaning 'to set down', 'to produce eggs'. Present tense *lay*; past tense *laid*; present participle *laying*; past participle *laid*. Examples:

I will lay a bet with you.   The hen laid an egg.
The hen was laying well.   The hen had laid an egg every day.

TO LIE: intransitive verb meaning 'to stretch out', 'to be recumbent'. Present tense *lie*; past tense *lay*; present participle *lying*; past participle *lain*. Examples:

I shall lie in bed until 10 o'clock.
We lay on the beach all the morning.
I was lying in bed when the doctor called.
I had lain in a coma for two days.

34. licence, license

The words *licence*, *advice* and *practice*, all ending in '-ce', are nouns.
The words *license*, *advise* and *practise*, all ending in '-se', are verbs.

I forgot to renew my television *licence*. (noun)
I must *license* my car next week. (verb)

I *practise* the violin for an hour every morning. (verb)
One hour's *practice* is not enough. (noun)

I shall *advise* my client to the best of my ability. (verb)
He charges a fee for his *advice*. (noun)

Note: The U.S. spelling is *license, practise* for both verb *and* noun.

35. like, as

In the context under consideration the word *like* is a preposition, and *as*
is a conjunction. Grammatically, prepositions precede nouns and
pronouns, and this applies to *like*. The word *as* is a subordinating
conjunction and is followed by an adverbial construction. Hence
educated practice and strict grammar declare these usages to be correct:

Right   He behaved like a madman.
Right   Why did you act like that?
Wrong   I went home like you did.
Right   Please do as I tell you.
Wrong   The price of food keeps going up like petrol does.
Wrong   It looks like it's going to rain.
Wrong   I go for a run every day like you do.

Most reputable English authorities call these 'wrong' usages either
illiterate or at least loose colloquialisms. In declaring them to be
'illiterate, vulgar and slovenly', Fowler urges conscientious writers to
avoid them. But it should be mentioned that in America *like* is
frequently used as a conjunction.

36. lose, loose

The word *lose* means to 'mislay' or 'be deprived of'. Verb only.

The word *loose* can be a verb or an adjective. *To loose* is a transitive
verb meaning 'to untie', 'to free'.

I hope I shan't *lose* my purse. (mislay; be deprived of)
My shoelace is *loose*. (untied)
Please *loose* this knot for me. (untie; make free)

37. me

Many young writers – and experienced ones – feel uncertain about the
use of this pronoun; in their concern to be correct and genteel they use 'I'
instead of 'me'. Study the following examples carefully:

Wrong The manager asked my wife and *I* out to dinner.

Wrong Between you and *I* there should be no secrets.

In both sentences *me* would be correct; in the first sentence because it is the object of the transitive verb 'invited', and in the second sentence because *me* is the form which follows a preposition.

In colloquial speech, however, we find that long custom has made the following acceptable: 'Who's there?' – 'It's all right; it's only *me*'; and 'He's taller than me.'

38. Mixed metaphors

Under 'Figures of Speech' (pp. 95–6) we shall discuss metaphors at some length. It is well to remember that in writing literary English you should not employ metaphors excessively, but those you use should be fresh and original as far as possible; never allow them to become mere clichés. At this point we are concerned with the danger of mixing metaphors. The following sentences illustrate the use of mixed metaphors. They should not be imitated.

At last the opposition's sacred cows have come home to roost.

The working class are the backbone of the nation; we must educate and train them and bring them to the front.

Gentlemen, I smell a rat; I see it hovering above our heads; if it is not promptly nipped in the bud, it will burst forth into a terrible conflagration that will deluge the world.

39. nice

Be very careful with this word. Avoid using it in loosely expressed phrases like 'a nice day'; 'a nice film'; 'a nice dinner' and so on. Always seek out the precise word – 'a warm, sunny day'; 'an exciting film'; 'a tasty and imaginative dinner'.

Remember, however, that *nice* has an exact meaning on occasions. We can properly say, 'He brought up a *nice* point in law.' This means a subtle, precise or delicate point in law. Or again, 'There is a *nice* distinction between being backward and being retarded.'

40. only

Watch carefully the placing of this adverb; it should be close to the word it modifies. Study these examples:

My sister *only* went shopping on Monday.

This has three possible meanings:

(*a*) Nobody other than my sister went shopping on Monday.

(*b*) My sister went out for the purpose of shopping and nothing else.

(*c*) My sister never shops on any day other than Monday.

To be clear you must write, '*Only* my sister went shopping on Monday', 'My sister went shopping on Monday *only*.'

If in doubt, it is wise to recast the sentence completely.

41. Past tense and past participle

A number of verbs such as 'to turn', 'to spell', 'to spill', 'to smell', 'to spoil' have alternative forms of the past tense and the past participle – 'burnt' and 'burned', 'spelt' and 'spelled' and so on – but there are some slight differences in usage.

(*a*) It is usual to write 'burnt', 'spoilt' when the verb is used transitively, as in 'He *burnt* his fingers.' The adjectival form is similarly 'A *burnt* offering'.

(*b*) The intransitive form usually employs the 'ed' ending, as in 'The building *burned* fiercely for six hours.'

42. principal, principle

These words are frequently confused, even by reputable writers.

Principal is often used as an adjective meaning 'chief, main, most important'. It is also a noun meaning the 'head of a college or school'. As a noun it can mean a sum of money which has been invested. Examples:

It is useful to know the *principal* parts of verbs.   (adj.)
The *Principal*, Dr John Webster, addressed the parents.   (noun)
The *principal* violinist in the orchestra was a German.   (adj.)
He received a good rate of interest on his *principal.*   (noun)

Principle is a noun meaning a 'general belief or truth', 'a law of nature', 'a rule used as a guide for action'. Examples:

The *principle* of freedom of speech is highly cherished by the democracies.
He is a man of high *principles.*
The *principle* of jet-propulsion has been known for many centuries; only its application is recent.

43. quite

Quite has two meanings. When it precedes gradable adjectives like 'good', 'bad', 'friendly', 'old', 'wide', it means 'fairly';

The book is quite good.   (i.e. not very good)
The new teacher is quite friendly.
I don't know his age but he seems quite old.

(Gradable adjectives are those which describe qualities which can exist in different measures; e.g. one person can be more or less friendly than another. Other adjectives cannot be graded; e.g. one person cannot be more or less dead than another.)

When 'quite' precedes non-gradable adjectives it means 'absolutely':

The young man was quite dead.
His command of the language is quite perfect.

44. Redundant adverbs

Many adverbs such as 'definitely' tend to be used carelessly and unnecessarily; they are words that can be profitably pruned away in accordance with George Orwell's advice: 'If it is possible to cut a word out, always cut it out.'

The most frequently abused adverbs are: *definitely*; *relatively*; *very*; *comparatively*; *unduly*; *actually*; *particularly*; *respectively*; *necessarily*; *hopefully*. Look at the following example:

Our special offer closes in a relatively short time.

These adverbs may rightly be used when something has been said or implied to give a standard of comparison; otherwise they are inclined to be redundant, tautological or meaningless, as our example above shows. It is arguable, however, that in statements like the following the use of *comparatively* is acceptable because there is a clear basis of comparison:

Of the eighty candidates, thirty were awarded passes and of these comparatively few were granted distinctions.

Even here Orwell's advice is appropriate.

45. Sequence of tenses

This term refers to the logical relationship in time between two or more tenses in a complex sentence (see p. 29). The correct usage can be simplified into two rules:

(1) A past tense in the main clause must be followed by a past tense in the subordinate clauses. For example:

He studied hard so that he might succeed.
I fully expected that he would come.
He told me he had to leave.

(2) A present or future tense in the main verb may be followed in the subordinate clauses by a verb in any tense. For example:

He tells me he has left school.
John says he will leave school next July.
I shall soon know if he is remaining in London.

There is one exception to the first rule, namely: if the subordinate clause following a main clause in the past tense expresses some universal or habitual fact, its verb can be in the present tense. Example:

These people did not seem to know that the earth moves round the sun.

46. Split infinitives

The construction termed 'split infinitive' consists of the separation of 'to' from the verb by the interposing of an adverb, as in the following:

He has a tendency *to loudly interrupt* any speaker who holds forth about the evils of tobacco.

Such sentences should be avoided in writing. The above could easily be rephrased as:

He has a tendency to interrupt loudly any speaker who holds forth about the evils of tobacco.

In the past, the splitting of an infinitive in any piece of writing was considered to be the ultimate literary sin. Today we look upon it more rationally, and hundreds of distinguished authors bear witness to this. We all agree that the aim of writing is to be clear, and if clarity is improved by a judiciously split infinitive, even Fowler condones it. He sums up the question in these words: 'Avoid the split infinitive wherever possible; but if it is the clearest and most natural construction, use it boldly. The angels are on our side.'

47. Tautology and repetition

Tautology is the unnecessary repetition of an idea or statement in different words. The fault appears in many forms. We have the simple and obvious, 'He sat alone on his own,' and 'This payment leaves me with only two pounds left.' We also meet expressions such as 'The reason he was late was because he overslept.' Here *the reason* and *because* duplicate the same idea. Again, many verbs occur with words and phrases which repeat, without augmenting, their meaning. The following examples illustrate this tendency and should not be imitated by the student:

ascend up	descend down	protrude out
classify into classes	final completion	repeat again
collaborate together	mix together	still continue
connect together	penetrate into	unite together

Some of these may be acceptable in colloquial speech, but they should not be used when serious or literary writing is being attempted.

Some further examples will show how easily the fault creeps in if a writer does not check and revise his work:

Occasionally the train was late, but *not very often.*
The thief took with him twenty bottles of expensive perfume and *substituted* empty bottles *in their place.*
The liner travelled at 20 knots *an hour.*
I could not *separate* the two twins *apart.*
The speaker *continued* to *remain* unmoved by the abuse.

Many doctors *seriously* maintain that excessive smoking is as *serious* as alcoholism.

I *regret* to say that many *regrettable* incidents took place.

He rose at 5.0 a.m. as was *frequently his custom.*

48. than

This word causes some difficulties as shown in the following:

(*a*) You gave him a better welcome *than I.* (gave him)

(*b*) You gave him a better welcome *than me.* (than you gave me)

In (*a*), *than* is a conjunction and it is best, on the whole, to complete the clause:

You gave him a better welcome than I did.

In (*b*), *than* is used as a preposition.

The use of *than* always involves a comparison:

He is taller than John.

He had no sooner arrived than he was called away again.

But, as we pointed out in item 27 above, ordinary adverbs of degree such as 'hardly', 'scarcely', 'barely', 'only', are followed by 'when'. For example:

Scarcely had the concert begun *when* there was a complete failure of the lights.

49. unique

This is a word to handle with care. It is an adjective meaning 'the only one of its kind, having no like or equal'. Hence there can be no degrees of uniqueness; a thing is either unique or it is not. Expressions such as 'very unique' or 'most unique' are wrong. It is possible, however, to say 'very rare' or 'very remarkable.'

50. Verbosity

This term may be defined as a superfluity of words; using more words than are necessary. This tendency often goes with a love of long words, high-sounding phrases and lengthy, complicated sentences. The fault may be seen in the use of prepositional phrases of various kinds, and in wordy, imprecise clauses that serve as mere padding. To some extent verbosity overlaps tautology.

Examples are prevalent in official reports and documents. Here are some specimens of various kinds; in general they should be avoided, though they may well be justifiable in certain contexts:

as regards	owing to the fact that
in connexion with	on the basis of
in relation to	in such time as

in the case of	cannot see the way clear to
with reference to	it is not inappropriate to mention
with regard to	it is appreciated that
in respect of	it should be noted that
as to whether	the committee will no doubt recollect that
in the last resort	it can be stated with some confidence that

On occasions some of these phrases can be very helpful in communicating a writer's meaning clearly, and so they must not be peremptorily discarded. The best advice is that writers should check and revise their work to see if unnecessary words and phrases can be eliminated. This way their meaning will be clear and their prose style interesting to read.

Exercises

Correct and explain any grammatical faults or errors of usage in the following:

1. Neither of the boys had completed their homework.
2. Magicians often show some remarkable allusions.
3. The reason he gave up football was because of a leg injury.
4. They must not expect you and me to join them.
5. His piano solo was chronic – the worst I have ever heard.
6. Can I borrow your bicycle tomorrow?
7. It was a period of continual drought; it lasted for six weeks.
8. He was elected to the town counsel.
9. Coming home late one night there was fearful accident.
10. The answer, which was given, was a flat refusal.
11. The Sahara dessert is a vast wilderness.
12. Alright, I will except your offer; it seems fair enough.
13. There were less than twenty people in the audience.
14. She was deeply effected by the sad news.
15. I can't except any advise from him.
16. I had scarcely sat down than the explosion occurred.
17. Its an ill advised plan.
18. There was a disturbing agitation for home-rule.
19. I felt that a disaster was eminent.
20. He was completely disinterested in football.
21. Its almost certain to rain tomorrow.
22. The boy is obedient; he invariably does like I say.
23. My best friend told my wife and I the sad news.
24. His report inferred that the bridge was dangerous.
25. The Statue of Liberty is very unique.

Part 3

The elements of composition

Sentences and clauses

There are three types of sentences in English: simple sentences, compound sentences and complex sentences.

Simple sentences

Simple sentences can appear in three main forms:

(1) John is ill.   The shops are shut.   The boys were friends.

This type consists of a *subject*, a *copulative verb* and a *complement*.

predicate

(2) David waited.   The game began.   The spectators cheered.

This type consists of a *subject* and an *intransitive verb*.

predicate

(3) Peter watched the match.   We beat the visitors.   The boys celebrated the victory.

This type consists of a *subject*, a *transitive verb* and an *object*.

predicate

The sentences quoted above are all statements – the most common kind of sentence; but there are two other kinds as well. The three kinds are:

Statement: The match was cancelled.
Question: Who cancelled it?
Command: Keep quiet!

Compound sentences

These are sentences which consist of two or more simple sentences joined together by such a co-ordinating conjunction as *and, but, so*:

My friend telephoned me and offered me a lift to the match.
He called at the house but I was out.
Take the first turn to the left, then drive on for two miles and then turn right.

Complex sentences

These are sentences which contain one or more subordinate clauses:

The man *who came to see me* stayed quite a long time *because he had a lot to say.*

Here we have the main part of the sentence 'The man . . . stayed quite a long time' and two subordinate parts. We have a subordinate adjective clause, 'who came to see me', and a subordinate adverb clause, 'because he had a lot to say'.

Expanders or modifiers

The three main forms of simple sentence mentioned above can all be expanded or modified by a word or words of an adjectival nature and by a word or words of an adverbial nature, as in the following examples:

(1) John is ill.

Poor John is *seriously* ill.
('Poor' is here an adjective: 'seriously' is an adverb.)

My youngest cousin John is seriously ill *with influenza.*
 (adjective phrase)   (adverb phrase)

(2) The game began.

The *exciting* game *then* began.
 (adjective)   (adverb)

The long-awaited game began *at 2.0 o'clock.*
(adjective phrase)   (adverb phrase)

(3) The boys celebrated the victory.

The *delighted* boys celebrated the victory *noisily.*
 (adjective)   (adverb)

The boys, *delighted with their success*, celebrated the victory
                     (adjective phrase)
with singing and dancing.
 (adverb phrase)

Adjective and adverb clauses

Expanders or modifiers may be adjective clauses or adverb clauses instead of phrases. Clauses have their own finite verbs, whereas phrases do not.

The following examples show how clauses derive, as it were, from the simple parts of speech:

The *table* lamp is lit.   (adjective)
The lamp *on the table* is lit.   (adjective phrase)
The lamp *which is on the table* is lit.   (adjective clause)

The accident happened *here.* (adverb)
The accident happened *on this spot.* (adverb phrase)
The accident happened *where I am standing.* (adverb clause)

Here are some examples of adjective and adverb clauses – subordinate or dependent clauses – within a main sentence:

(1) My youngest cousin, John, *who is on holiday with us,* is seriously ill with influenza, *because he was soaked to the skin in the storm.*

Here 'who is on holiday with us' is an adjective clause describing John (finite verb 'is'); and 'because he was soaked to the skin in yesterday's storm' is an adverb clause (finite verb 'was soaked'), expanding the predicate.

(2) The exciting game, *which we had long been anticipating,* began *when the clock struck two.*

Here is an adjective clause describing 'game' (finite verb 'had been anticipating') and an adverb clause (finite verb 'struck'), expanding the predicate.

(3) The delighted boys, *who were thrilled with their success,* celebrated the victory *when they arrived home.*

Here we have an adjective clause describing the boys, and an adverb clause, expanding the predicate.

Types of adverb clause
The clauses that tend to appear most frequently in any passage of prose are adverbial. Here is a list of the nine types of adverb clauses, together with some of the links (subordinating conjunctions) that introduce them:

1. Time	when, while, before, after, as, since
2. Place	where
3. Manner	as
4. Degree	as
5. Condition	if, if not, unless
6. Concession	although, though, even though
7. Consequence	so that
8. Purpose	in order that, so that
9. Reason	because, as, since

All these types of adverb clause expand the meaning of the verb in the main part of the sentence, as in the following:

I went into town *when I had finished my breakfast.* (adverb clause of time)
My brother could not go with me *because he was ill.* (adverb clause of reason)

If he is better tomorrow he will be able to go out again.   (adverb clause of condition)

Sometimes the same link can introduce different kinds of clause. For example:

Since he was ill he could not play.
(reason – tells us *why*)

Since I went to Spain last summer I have been learning Spanish.
(time – tells us *how long*)

As the old man was walking down the street, he was attacked.
(time – tells us *when*)

As he was old and feeble he could not defend himself.
(reason – tells us *why*)

Noun clauses

While adjective and adverb phrases and clauses are the most common expanders or modifiers, noun phrases and noun clauses can also function in a similar manner. Look carefully at the following examples:

His *reply* was unexpected.	Noun as subject
What he said in reply was unexpected.	Noun clause as subject
I heard his *comment*.	Noun as object
I heard *what he said*.	Noun clause as object
I listened to his *reply*.	Noun as object of preposition *to*
I listened to *what he said in reply*.	Noun clause as object of preposition *to*

The secret of variety

These methods of expanding or modifying simple sentences give you the secret of writing mature English prose. The use of clauses as expanders allows you to write complex sentences (which by definition must contain one or more subordinate clauses), and these are established features of most sophisticated or literary writing. By ringing the changes on your expanders and modifiers, sometimes using simple adjectives and adverbs or the same type of phrases, and at other times using similar clauses – and also noun clauses – you can achieve a pleasing variety in your sentences.

There is no question of one type of expander being 'better' than another, but it is wise not to jostle together too many subordinate clauses in the same long complex sentence. If in doubt 'stop and start again' with a new sentence, remembering that there is much virtue in simplicity and brevity.

Exercises

1. Which of the following are statements, questions or commands?

   (*a*) He lived to a ripe old age.
   (*b*) How old is he?
   (*c*) Old age catches up on all of us.
   (*d*) Come home at once!

2. Which of the following are complex sentences?

   (*a*) Angered by his treatment, the young man went to the manager of the hotel and complained bitterly about the staff's behaviour.
   (*b*) Arriving late at the party, John looked for his host, but was unable to find him in the crush.
   (*c*) Towards the end of the evening John found his host who was playing cards in the playroom with some of his friends.

3. Re-write the following sentence, substituting a *phrase* for each of the words in italic:

   The *talented* footballer scored goals *regularly*.

   Now re-write the sentence again, this time substituting a *clause* for each of the words in italic. Example:

   The *skilful* carpenter *quickly* made a kennel for the dog.
   The carpenter, *a man of considerable skill*, made a dog-kennel *in a very short time*. (phrases)
   The carpenter, *who was a craftsman of considerable skill*, had finished making a kennel for the dog *before he took his mid-day break*. (clauses)

4. Replace the nouns printed in italic with noun clauses (having their own finite verb. Examples:

   He was pleased with his *success*. He was pleased that he had succeeded.
   The little girl showed her *sadness*. The little girl showed that she was sad.

   (*a*) The boy was praised for his *effort*.
   (*b*) The prisoner was hoping for *justice*.
   (*c*) Nobody accepted his *explanation*.
   (*d*) He annoyed his parents by his *refusal*.
   (*e*) John was disappointed by the committee's *decision*.

5. Re-write the following sentences, replacing the expressions printed in italic with adverbial clauses. (If necessary you can refer back to the list of adverbial clauses):

(a) *At the conclusion of the concert* the applause was deafening.
(b) *The captain's illness* caused the postponement of the game.
(c) *In spite of the postponement* the game will definitely be played later.
(d) I shall wait *for his arrival.*
(e) *By locking* your bicycle you will prevent thieves from stealing it.

6. Re-write the following sentences, replacing the expressions printed in italic either with a single word or with a phrase:

(a) The team *who challenged us* arrived by coach.
(b) Half-time will be indicated *when the referee blows his whistle.*
(c) *When the game started* we certainly hoped *we would win.*
(d) The two players *who were injured* were given treatment by the doctor *who was on duty.*

7. Using the following sentence:

Starving peasants will *invariably* revolt.

write two further sentences, (a) substituting phrases for the words in italic; (b) substituting clauses for the words in italic.

How to write clearly

The unit of composition is the sentence which, as we have seen, can be simple, compound or complex.

All prose writing consists of sentences of these various kinds. By following certain principles we can be more likely to express ourselves clearly, and these principles concern both the individual words that combine to make a sentence and the structure of the sentences themselves. Here are the principles:

(1) Do not put two or more related ideas in a sentence separated only by a comma. Either start a new sentence or, if there is a logical connexion between them, make the second sentence a subordinate clause that brings out the connexion.

Wrong   I went to London by train last Thursday, my married daughter came up from Dover to meet me.

Right   Last Thursday I went by train to London where I was met by my daughter from Dover.

(2) Avoid long complicated sentences in which it is difficult to follow the meaning. Conversely, avoid too many short, snappy sentences such as young children tend to write. Think out your logical connexions and try to vary your sentence structures. The following example shows how to deal with a series of short sentences:

Wrong   I telephoned you last Saturday. You specially asked me to do this. You were not at your office nor at home. On Monday I rang up again. Fortunately your secretary was in the office. She was able to give me the information. I wanted it urgently.

Right   As requested, I telephoned you on Saturday, but you were not at the office nor at home, so I decided to ring you up on Monday. Fortunately your secretary was in the office and she was able to give me the information that I needed so urgently.

Here the linking words are 'As', 'but', 'so', 'and', 'that'.

(3) Vary the form of your sentences., You have seen in the preceding paragraph how you can link your ideas together by using appropriate phrases and clauses. Next you should consider how you can get variety in your writing by using different types of sentence structures, for example by constructing some of your sentences as 'loose' sentences, and others as 'periodic' sentences.

Loose sentences are built up in the normal fashion of subject, verb and modifier, when the meaning is more or less clear before you reach the end. Periodic sentences, on the other hand, are inverted, with the modifier coming before the verb. In these instances the meaning of the sentence is not clear until it is 'clinched' by the appearance of the verb at the end. Here are two examples of typical periodic sentences:

> After months of despair and false hopes, at the very end of December, came news of the relief party.
>
> To those who work conscientiously for many years, success will at last come.

Further variety and interest can be achieved by using occasional short sentences, or by employing a sharp contrast or antithesis. The latter is somewhat artificial but it is effective if used with discretion:

> Although Peter had an easy-going nature, he could be determined and disciplined in an emergency.
>
> The more he spent on his hobby, the less he had for his family.

(4) Do not change your viewpoint or your constructions. Study the following:

Wrong	I like my uncle because of his cheerful nature and because he is generous to me.
Right	I like my uncle because of his cheerful nature and because of his generosity to me.
Wrong	Last night I did some intensive reading, after which some serious writing was attempted.
Right	Last night I did some intensive reading and then attempted some serious writing.

(5) Do not mix active and passive voices, and remember that the active voice is often the more vivid and immediate. Use it in preference to the passive. Study the following examples:

Avoid	The producer staged a play of rare distinction, and the critics of London and New York were evidently impressed by him.
Better	The producer staged a play of rare distinction and clearly impressed the critics of London and New York.
Avoid	It was decided by the Inspector of police that a house-to-house search should be undertaken, and ten constables were immediately despatched to commence this assignment.
Better	The Inspector of police decided to carry out a house-to-house search, and immediately sent ten constables to do this.

These examples illustrate many of the points mentioned earlier, not only the rule about actives and passives.

(6) Watch your vocabulary carefully:

(*a*) Use familiar and short words rather than erudite, long ones.

(*b*) Use concrete words rather than abstract ones.

These recommendations really overlap as these examples show:

Wrong   Continual vigilance by the public is imperative.

Right   We must always be on the watch.

Wrong   The construction of an acoustically conceived auditorium for the presentation of contemporary experimental orchestral compositions as well as of traditional ones is at present under active consideration.

Right   The building of a well-designed hall for concerts of modern and classical music is now being considered.

Wrong   An amelioration of domiciliary facilities is an admitted priority.

Right   First we need to build better houses.

Exercises

1. State whether the following are simple, compound or complex sentences:

   (*a*) He started to read a novel but gave it up after two hours.

   (*b*) He could never settle down for long as he was restless by nature.

   (*c*) After breakfast he went to the shops to buy more food.

   (*d*) When he had finished this task he went home with his purchases.

   (*e*) As he entered the room he was jumped upon by the intruder.

   (*f*) After he had written his letters he went to bed.

2. Re-write (*a*) as one sentence, and (*b*) as two sentences:

   (*a*) In 1979 I visited Venice. It is at the head of the Adriatic sea. The city is ancient and of unsurpassed beauty. Nearly all the thoroughfares are waterways. The canals are very fine.

   (*b*) Many cruise liners visit the Mediterranean. There are so many historic places to visit. Some of the liners call at Crete, Athens and Venice. Others visit islands such as Mykonos, Lesbos, Rhodes and Cyprus – sometimes calling at Istanbul and Alexandria as well.

3. The clarity of the following sentences is impaired by a simple fault in composition in each case. Re-write the sentences correctly.

   (*a*) I enjoy visiting London because of its many historic buildings and because it has such a great variety.

   (*b*) My friend and I caught the underground train to Trafalgar Square, and then a coach took us to the Tower of London.

   (*c*) The reason we visited the Tower was because we wanted to see the Crown Jewels and other treasures.

(d) All together we spent a whole morning on the historic site.
(e) Proceeding down towards the river the famous Traitors' Gate could be seen.
(f) As a result of an office blunder the market gardener now has about two tons of pig manure on his hands.
(g) The entertainments committee will hold an enquiry on beach donkeys at 2.0 p.m. in the main hall.
(h) The subject of the lecture was about atoms in industry.
(i) The two first boys home in the marathon were Smith and Jones.

The paragraph

We have seen that the sentence is the basic unit of expression, and that it can take various forms. A series of sentences can combine to form a paragraph, which is the next stage in expression. Such a collection of sentences must have a recognisable structure and unity, for it is this feature that gives validity to the paragraph. A sustained composition will consist of a series of paragraphs, and if the composition has been well thought out, the paragraphs will tend to separate and identify themselves quite naturally.

In his zeal to preserve unity, a writer may construct an unduly long paragraph, but it will be advantageous to break it down into two or even three shorter paragraphs. This can be done without sacrificing the impression of unity, provided there are appropriate link words or phrases that clearly associate the second and third paragraphs with the main theme or topic embodied in the first.

The use of short paragraphs

Very short sentences and paragraphs can make the writing vivid and arresting, but if used to excess they tend to create a journalistic style rather than a literary one. If the writer is aiming at an audience that favours a sharp journalistic style, then the use of frequent short sentences and paragraphs is undoubtedly justified. Short paragraphs certainly help to break up a solid page of print, and this on occasions is very desirable, as nothing is more deadening and intimidating than to be faced with a seemingly unending wall of words.

By reading the works of good, lively writers, and by assiduously practising the writing of continuous prose, the student will gradually acquire a feeling for the effective use of language, and it is from this that his judgment, taste and sense of style will develop.

Paragraphing by Dickens

Charles Dickens provides us with admirable examples of the art of paragraphing. His novels are very long and Dickens employs description extensively to set the scene and to build up atmosphere. But he breaks up his prose by frequent new paragraphs and, of course, by dialogue. At the moment we are concerned with the former which we shall illustrate by an extract from *Oliver Twist*. At this point in the story Oliver has been forced to take part in a burglary late one winter night. The burglars are discovered and Oliver suffers quite a severe gunshot wound. His evil companions make their escape carrying the injured Oliver with them, but as he hinders their flight they throw him, unconscious, into a ditch.

Here is the extract with the paragraphs numbered:

OLIVER IS INJURED AND ABANDONED

(1) The air grew colder, as the day came slowly on; and the mist rolled along the ground like a dense cloud of smoke. The grass was wet; the pathways, and low places, were all mire and water; the damp breath of an unwholesome wind went languidly by, with a hollow moaning. Still, Oliver lay motionless and insensible on the spot where Sikes had left him.

(2) Morning drew on apace. The air became more sharp and piercing, as its first dull hue – the death of night, rather than the birth of day – glimmered faintly in the sky. The objects which had looked dim and terrible in the darkness, grew more and more defined, and gradually resolved into their familiar shapes. The rain came down, thick and fast, and pattered noisily among the leafless bushes. But Oliver felt it not, as it beat against him; for he lay stretched, helpless and unconscious, on his bed of clay.

(3) At length, a low cry of pain broke the stillness that prevailed; and uttering it, the boy awoke. His left arm, rudely bandaged in a shawl, hung heavy and useless at his side: the bandage was saturated with blood. He was so weak, that he could scarcely raise himself into a sitting posture; when he had done so, he looked feebly around for help, and groaned with pain. Trembling in every joint, from cold and exhaustion, he made an effort to stand upright; but, shuddering from head to foot, fell prostrate on the ground.

(4) After a short return of the stupor in which he had been so long plunged, Oliver, urged by a creeping sickness at his heart, which seemed to warn him that if he lay there, he must surely die, got upon his feet, and essayed to walk. His head was dizzy, and he staggered to and fro like a drunken man. But he kept on, nevertheless, and, with his head drooping languidly on his breast, went stumbling onward, he knew not whither.

The above extract is a good example of how paragraphs seem to separate themselves almost naturally, as has been mentioned earlier. The four paragraphs represent distinct stages of a developing sequence, forming a coherent unity in total:

Paragraph 1 tells of the cold hours of darkness, when Oliver lay in the ditch, half frozen and insensible.

Paragraph 2 leads on naturally, closely linked by the sentence 'Morning drew on apace.' The air is piercingly cold as the first glimmer of the dawn appears.

Paragraph 3 is linked to the sequence of events by the phrase 'At length' and tells of Oliver's agonising return to consciousness and his struggle to stand on his own feet, only to collapse to the ground.

Paragraph 4 records the final stage, linked by the phrase 'After a short return of the stupor . . .', in which he makes a last desperate attempt to survive as he struggles to his feet and staggers blindly to seek help.

The whole passage could have been written as one long paragraph, but by breaking it up into four short sections the sequence of events is more clear-cut and is easier to read.

Notice, incidentally, that Dickens punctuates in the manner of his time, using far more commas than we would today.

More examples to study

(a) If we turn to the extract from *Gulliver's Travels* on pp. 108–9 we can see how Swift plans his paragraphs:

Paragraph 1 introduces us in general to the emperor's entertainments, which the author promises to describe in detail.

Paragraph 2 gives us a detailed account of the rope-dancers.

Paragraph 3 tells us of the frequent accidents that occur.

Paragraph 4 proceeds to tell us of the next entertainment – the leaping and creeping competition.

In this extract we have a sequence of events, introduced by a general comment and described in separate paragraphs. There is nothing profound in the art of paragraphing; it merely requires orderly thinking and taking care to group separate aspects or topics together, proceeding from the general to the particular.

(b) Now turn to the extract from Addison's *Spectator* on pp. 109–11. This author's style is polished and elegant. His paragraphs are generally on the long side and are carefully and artfully constructed. He is deliberately wooing his cultivated audience and his vocabulary is self-conscious and erudite, as is evident in words such as 'speculation', 'transient', 'intermittent', 'equipage', 'conduce' and 'exalted'. His paragraphing, however, is logical and coherent; he builds up his persuasive argument in three stages, beginning with a general statement, and turning to particular topics in the succeeding paragraphs:

Paragraph 1 allows Addison to point out, in general terms, the wide and growing appeal of his paper, and to give an undertaking to entertain and improve his readers.

Paragraph 2 proceeds from the general to the particular, and Addison recommends his paper as regular reading for all well-regulated families, because of its recreational and civilising appeal. He neatly links this paragraph to the first in the opening sentence.

Paragraph 3 shows how Addison narrows down his target still further; he particularly recommends his writing to the 'female world'.

Each paragraph covers a clear, identifiable topic and develops naturally from its predecessor.

(c) Next turn to the extracts from Stevenson on pp. 111–13.

The first extract consists of one complete paragraph. It opens with a general statement, his dreamlike descent, which sums up all that follows – the changing terrain, and the ever-changing character of the stream as it tumbles and cascades down to the inviting pools at the bottom of the valley. This is a good example of a paragraph building up to a cumulative unity, as it describes the brisk descent from the stark, rocky summit to the crystal-green pools in the meadow below. As a paragraph it fulfils the strictest criteria of excellence, as it begins with a compelling opening sentence and ends with a climax of pure physical delight.

In Stevenson's second extract we have a further example of effective paragraphing. Here we need only concern ourselves with his opening paragraph, for it is an almost perfect example of what a paragraph should be. In it Jim Hawkins provides us with our first clear description of the island, following the brief glimpse by moonlight the night before.

The paragraph begins with Jim Hawkins noticing the different impression of the island, as compared with the romantic, moon-lit landfall he experienced the previous night. The changed appearance is sketched out for us step by step – the grey-coloured woods in the foreground dappled by streaks of yellow sand, and further back the tall pine trees leading to the rising hills which soon turned to rocky outcrops and dominated by the stark Spy-glass hill which was 'suddenly cut off at the top like a pedestal to put a statue on'.

In this paragraph we have the general pointer of the opening sentence – the sense of change. Then the details are sketched in, from the foreground to the background, ever rising up until the rocky, pedestal-like summit of Spy-glass is reached. Such a climactic ending is the ideal conclusion for every paragraph, but it is not always possible for the average writer to fashion his paragraphs in this way.

Part 4

Punctuation and spelling

P<small>UNCTUATION AND SPELLING</small> are basically matters of custom and good manners. They are both aspects of English usage that are based on history, convention and habit, but they make a genuine contribution to clear and unambiguous expression. For this reason they must be taken seriously.

A guide to punctuation

In the writing of English our prime concern must always be for clarity. Punctuation, as we shall see, can contribute to this and, along with considerations of grammar and usage in general, it plays an essential part in English expression. Today we are far less fussy about punctuation than we were fifty or more years ago when writers tended to over-punctuate. This tendency was even more pronounced further back still, as we can see if we refer to the extracts from the works of Defoe and Swift, quoted in a later section. There still are today a few simple rules to be strictly observed, but we are entitled to a certain amount of discretion provided clarity is not sacrificed.

There are nine punctuation marks to be studied carefully; these are as follows:

1. The full stop (or period)

This stop is used to indicate the end of a sentence. Examples:

This is the road to London.
It is well known that lead paint is poisonous.

The full stop is also used after abbreviations. Examples:

U.S.A.   U.K.   e.g. (*exempli gratia* – for example)
M. (Monsieur)   a.m.   p.m.

But where the abbreviation ends with the last letter of the original word, no full stop is considered necessary today, even though it formerly was required. Examples: Mr   Mrs   Dr   St (Saint).

Certain familiar abbreviations are also becoming accepted without any full stops, for example, UNESCO, NATO. Such abbreviations are often pronounced as words and are called 'acronyms'.

2. The colon

This stop indicates a substantial pause, yet suggests a close connexion between the parts of the sentence so separated. Its most common use is to introduce lists or a series of items, as if it meant 'namely', as in these examples:

> The following boys and girls were awarded prizes: George Welby, Peter Smale, Wendy Evett, Edward Townley, Jane Dix, Paul Lewis and Roger Johnson.
> The tunic is available in many materials: wool, cotton, nylon and terylene.

A second use of the colon is to make an emphatic contrast between two ideas in a sentence; in this it is stronger than a semicolon.

> In England licensing hours are rigidly controlled: on the continent alcoholic drinks are available at any hour of the day.
> The committee began its work in a spirit of hope and optimism: it ended it in disillusion and despair.

Colons are also often used to introduce quotations.

> As Shakespeare said: 'What's in a name?'

3. Semicolon

This stop indicates a pause that is shorter than a colon but longer than a comma. It is frequently used to link clauses that are grammatically complete but very closely related in meaning.

> The match, regrettably, had to be cancelled; this was the wisest decision in the circumstances.
> If you opt for German, please inform Mr Rowlands; if you choose Spanish, please see Miss Ramirez.

Another valuable use of the semicolon is to express a sharp, dramatic contrast, which is not however complete enough to justify using a colon:

> In panic he dashed down the other tunnel; it was blocked too.
> His tackling was devastating; three of his opponents were carried off on stretchers.

4. The comma

The comma is chiefly used to indicate a slight pause in a sentence, just as we naturally pause in our speech to make our meaning clear. There are a few rigid rules. Commas must be employed to separate lists of nouns or phrases in apposition (that is, side by side), for example:

> He spoke a surprising number of languages: English, French, German, Italian and Spanish.
> Captain Lucas, the pilot of the plane, called the control tower on his radio.

The new model will give a better mileage to the gallon, more lively acceleration, a smoother suspension and more efficient braking.

Again, a pair of commas must be employed to mark off a comment or an aside that breaks into the continuity of a sentence. For example:

Our performance, as you know, drew packed houses for a month.

Our aim at all times must be to be clear and unambiguous, hence we can recognise the importance of the commas, or the absence of them, in the following sentences:

The witness, said the policeman, was not telling the truth.
The witness said the policeman was not telling the truth.

Another obligatory use of commas occurs with certain adjectival clauses. These can be of two types – one defines the subject more closely; the other is non-defining or commenting, that is, it adds something new. Study carefully the following examples:

The visitor *who called* was a native of Peru.
The man *who sold the car* was a rogue.

The above are defining adjective clauses and need no commas.

The letter, *which incidentally was delivered by hand,* was abusive.
The driver, *who did not have an insurance policy,* admitted his responsibility for the accident.

Here we have commenting or non-defining adjective clauses which need to be placed between commas; they add something new and might even have been placed between brackets.

Having looked at the more obligatory use of commas, we can now study examples in which we have to rely more on our judgment. For instance, commas are advisable to mark off long subordinate clauses that precede a main clause, as in the following example:

After a very successful meeting had been held by the executive committee to decide on the company's future policy, a full report of the proceedings was presented to the meeting of shareholders.

When the sentence is short its meaning is usually immediately apparent, so no comma is necessary, as in the following example:

If I am late please start without me.

On the other hand some short sentences can pose a slight problem:

When you are standing below the statue appears huge.

When you read this sentence quickly, as in ordinary reading, it may appear to be a little muddled, causing you to read it through again. This slight difficulty is at once removed by the use of an appropriate comma:

When you are standing below, the statue appears huge.

5. Question mark (or mark of interrogation)

This is used only for direct questions:

> What is the time, please?
> Which is the platform for the London trains?

Question marks are never used in reported or indirect speech:

> He asked his friend what the time was.

Sometimes a written sentence may not look like a question, but in speaking it the tone of voice would immediately convey the sense of a question:

> It really was Peter's own fault?

Conversely, with rhetorical questions, the sentences look like questions but have the value of emphatic statements:

> Do you believe we would break our word?
>   (i.e. Surely you know we would not break our word?)
> Is there a sane person anywhere who does not want peace?

6. Exclamation mark

Excessive use of exclamation marks reveals the uneducated and unskilled writer. Like strychnine in medicine it is good if used sparingly and with discretion. Exclamation marks should be used as follows:

(*a*) After single-word exclamations or interjections:
>   Oh!   Wait!   Stop!

(*b*) After brief phrases used as interjections:
>   Good Lord!   Heavens above!

(*c*) In short sentences containing an exclamatory 'How' or 'What':
>   What I have suffered!   How I detest the fellow!

(*d*) In short sentences expressing a feeling or wish:
>   God forbid!   May we never live to see that day!

(*e*) Elliptical (i.e. shortened) phrases expressing strong feelings:
>   You little rat!   You dirty dog!

From the above you can see that we usually employ exclamation marks after expressions that are not complete sentences. On certain occasions however, we can use an exclamation mark at the end of a complete sentence to convey the feeling or tone of voice behind it:

> You thought you could get away with it!
> The culprit was his own brother!

The golden rule is *Use exclamation marks sparingly.*

7. Quotation marks (or inverted commas)

You can use either single or double inverted commas to denote the actual words used by a speaker. (In this book single ones have been used.) They are placed at the beginning and end of the spoken words in direct speech only. Study the following example closely, and notice how ordinary commas and full stops are used in the passage:

> The blind man pulled me close up to him.
> 'Now, boy,' he said, 'take me in to the captain.'
> 'Sir,' said I, 'upon my word I dare not.'
> 'Oh,' he sneered, 'that's it. Take me in straight, or I'll break your arm.'
> And he gave it, as he spoke, a wrench that made me cry out.
> 'Sir,' I said, 'it is for yourself I mean. The captain is not what he used to be. He sits with a drawn cutlass. Another gentleman . . .'
> 'Come, now, march,' interrupted he; and I never heard a voice so cruel, and cold, and ugly as that blind man's.

It is possible that there may be a quotation *within* a passage of direct speech. If you are using single inverted commas, the quotation can be indicated by double ones, as in this example:

> At this point young Jim Hawkins spoke up.
> 'I tell you, Dr Livesey, the blind rogue threatened me, saying, "Take me in straight, or I'll break your arm." I had no alternative but to obey.'

Similarly, if you are using double inverted commas, the quotation can be indicated by single ones.

8. Parenthesis
This is the use of brackets or dashes to mark out a comment or explanation that is not grammatically part of the rest of the sentence. For example:

> The report clearly states (see page 33) that the chairman had to leave the meeting at this critical point.
> The explanation – as I mentioned at the time – was perfectly clear and intelligible.

9. The apostrophe
The apostrophe is represented by a comma above the line; it indicates either an omitted letter or a possessive case. Here it indicates an omitted letter:

> It's cold to-day.   ('It's' stands for 'It is')
> I don't know.   (here the letter 'o' in 'not' has been omitted)
> There's a taxi over there. (the letter 'i' has been omitted from 'is')

The use of the apostrophe to indicate the possessive is a little more difficult. The general rule is to add an apostrophe 's' to signify possession in a singular noun. For example:

The dog's kennel.   Jane's doll   The pilot's name.

If, however, the plural form of the noun ends in the letter 's', then the possessive case is shown by adding an apostrophe *after* the final 's':

The boys' desks totalled twenty-four.
The horses' stables were gutted by fire.
The umpires' white coats were missing.

Plural nouns that do *not* end in 's' form the possessive by adding an apostrophe 's', as in the following:

The men's work was completed in two hours.
The children's toys were very realistic.

With proper names that end in 's' it is customary to form the possessive by adding an apostrophe and another 's':

Charles's idea   St Thomas's Hospital   Dylan Thomas's poems
Mr Jones's family   Pythagoras's theorems

Care must be taken not to confuse *it's* (it is) and *its* (possessive adjective) – see item 32, p.20 above.

Capital letters

The first word of a sentence must begin with a capital letter. Capital letters are also used for:

(*a*) all proper names; for example, Peter, Mary, Jenkins, London, France. Geographical names consisting of two words should have a capital for each: for example, River Mersey, Ozark Mountains.

(*b*) the first word in direct speech, as in: He asked, 'Where are you going?'

(*c*) the days of the week and the months of the year.

(*d*) titles and names of organisations; for example: St Mary, Dr Smith, Mr Brown, Lord Quex, the Duke of Buckingham, the Ministry of Defence.

(*e*) the first and other important words in the titles of books, plays, films and so on: for example, *A Journal of the Plague Year*, *Around the World in Eighty Days*.

Exercises

1. Punctuate the following and change small letters to capitals where necessary:

   pushing a trolley mary made her way through the supermarket buying strictly according to her shopping list in the middle aisle she caught sight of her friend pamela hello pam she called out wait for me at the door as you go out right answered pam but dont be too long ive got to call to see my dentist at 11 oclock thats all right replied mary i wont keep you waiting

2. Write three sentences showing how the proper use of the semicolon can add vividness and dramatic quality to your expression.

3. Punctuate the following, using single inverted commas to denote the speakers and changing small letters to capitals where necessary. To make your answer clear, begin each speaker's remarks on a new line.

   whats your name sir inquired the judge sam weller my lord replied the gentleman do you spell it with a v or a w inquired the judge that depends upon the taste and fancy of the speller my lord replied sam i never had occasion to spell it more than once or twice in my life but i spells it with a v here a voice in the gallery exclaimed aloud quite right too samivel quite right put it down a we my lord put it down a we who is that that dares to address the court said the little judge looking up usher yes my lord bring that person here instantly yes my lord

4. Punctuate the following and change small letters to capitals where necessary:

   from the chemists shop my brother edward a hypochondriac if ever there was one bought a packet of cold-tablets a tin of throat pastilles two bottles of aspirins actually aspros a small jar of vitamin tablets and some cotton wool

5. Punctuate the following and change small letters to capitals where necessary:

   (a) the new conductor dr panolski who took over the orchestra was originally a talented violinist he specialised in the music of bach

   (b) the guest of honour whose home town was bristol was a writer of some distinction

   (c) tomorrow if i am home in time i shall give a special present to the boy who delivers the morning papers

   (d) i once met a man who had seen a flying saucer if we are to believe what he said

   (e) the rumour however that he had actually seen its crew was soon vehemently denied this is the official police version

6. Punctuate and set out correctly the following parts of a letter:
   (a) *Your own address*: bryony cottage 14 the esplanade dawlish devon
   (b) *The evelope*: henry joberns castle view upper high street brighton sussex

7. Show the correct use of the apostrophe in the following, re-writing them as necessary:
   (a) the bone of one dog
   (b) the bones of more than one dog
   (c) the cloakroom of the ladies
   (d) the dressing room of the men
   (e) the cat had liver for . . . . . . breakfast.   (it's or its?)
   (f) Here comes the train: . . . . . . certain to be full.   (it's or its?)
   (g) Good; . . . . . . early today.   (it's or its?)
   (h) The train has lost . . . . . . guard's van.   (it's or its?)
   (i) . . . . . . coupling must have broken.   (it's or its?)

8. Re-write the following, giving the exact words you think the speakers would have used, and retaining the background information. Use single inverted commas to denote the speakers, thus converting a passage of indirect speech to direct speech:

   My friend John called to me across the street, rather urgently, I thought. I waved back and walked across to ask him what the trouble was. He told me that news had just come in that our date of sailing had been brought forward by a week. When I expressed my surprise he reminded me that the travel agent had warned us of the possibility. I asked him if he knew the reason for the change. John replied that he understood it was because of the threatened dock strike at Southampton.

9. Re-write the following passage in reported or indirect speech:

   'Keep indoors, men,' said the captain. 'Ten to one this is a trick.' Then he hailed the buccaneer.
   'Who goes there? Stand, or we fire.'
   'Flag of truce,' cried Silver.
   Captain Smollett turned and spoke to us:
   'Dr Livesey, take the north side, if you please; Jim, the east; Gray, west. All hands to load muskets. Lively, men, and careful.'
   And then he turned again to the mutineers.
   'And what do you want with your flag of truce?' he cried.
   'Cap'n Silver, sir, to come on board and make terms,' was the reply.

A guide to spelling

Whatever developments the future may bring in the way of word-processors and other microchip magic, the ability to spell correctly will always be a valuable asset. It is true that many writers have found difficulty with modern English spelling conventions but students must always endeavour to learn the rules that govern English spelling as well as the exceptions to the rules. The following points may prove useful:

(1) Many English words change their spelling before the endings '-ing', '-ed', '-er' and '-est', thus:

bat	batting, batted	fit	fitter, fittest

The consonant is *not* doubled when:

(*a*) the word ends in a vowel:

hate	hating, hated	safe	safer, safest

(*b*) the word ends in two consonants:

last	lasting, lasted	fast	faster, fastest

(*c*) the final syllable is not stressed:

brighten   brightening   (the stress falls on the first syllable)

(2) In British English, final 'l' is always doubled:

marvel marvelling, marvelled   cancel cancelling, cancelled

In American English, the 'l' is only doubled if it occurs in the stressed syllable:

propel	propelling, propelled (Br. *and* U.S.)
	(stress falls on second syllable)
travel	traveled (U.S.), travelled (Br.)
	(stress falls on first syllable)

(3) Final 'y' changes to 'i' before word endings like '-ed', '-er', and to 'ies' in the formation of third persons and plurals:

early	earlier, earliest
funny	funnier, funniest, funnily
carry	carries, carried, carriage
rely	relied, reliable, reliant
story	stories
entry	entries

Final 'y' does not change to 'i' if

(*a*) the 'y' follows a vowel:

buy buying, buyer   say sayings   donkey donkeys

or:

(*b*) the ending begins with 'i':

    dry   drying   study   studying   essay   essayist

(4) Final 'ie' changes to 'y' before 'ing':

    die   dying   lie   lying

(5) When the letters 'i' and 'e' occur together and are pronounced like *ee*, the 'i' *precedes* the 'e'. Examples:

    field   niece   pier

When these letters follow 'c', however, the 'e' *precedes* the 'i'. Examples:

    deceive   receive   ceiling

The exception to this rule ('i' before 'e' except after 'c') is 'seize'.

N.B. There are a number of words where 'e' precedes 'i' and where the 'ei' is pronounced like *ay* (as in 'day'). Examples:

    beige   veil   reign

The formation of plurals

(1) Most nouns form plurals by adding 's':

    dog   dogs   chair   chairs   book   books

(2) If the root ends in 's', 'x', 'ch' or 'o', the plural requires 'es':

    loss   losses   fox   foxes   church churches
    dish   dishes   potato potatoes   echo echoes

Exceptions:

    solo   solos   folio   folios   canto   cantos
    studio studios   piano   pianos   photo   photos

(3) When a noun ends in 'y', you usually change the 'y' into 'i' and add 'es' – provided the letter before the 'y' is a consonant:

    fly   flies   berry   berries   cry   cries

Exceptions (*when the 'y' is preceded by a vowel*):

    day days   monkey monkeys   valley valleys
    journey journeys   alloy alloys   kidney kidneys

(4) When a noun ends in 'f', or 'fe', you usually change the 'f' into 'v' and add 'es':

    loaf   loaves   knife   knives   leaf   leaves
    wife   wives   thief   thieves   calf   calves

Exceptions:

chief	chiefs	roof	roofs	reef	reefs
grief	griefs	gulf	gulfs	belief	beliefs

A very few words may have either form:

hoof	hoofs *or* hooves	scarf	scarfs *or* scarves

(5) Notice the rules for the plurals of compound and hyphenated words:

(*a*)   the more important word is made plural. For example, 'court martial' becomes 'courts martial'. (Note that the noun form has no hyphen but the verb form has – 'to court-martial')

(*b*)   if the two parts are joined into one word, without a hyphen, then it is treated as a single word:

spoonful	spoonfuls	dairymaid	dairymaids
candlestick	candlesticks		

But in a very few cases both parts of the word are made plural: for example, 'manservant' becomes 'menservants'.

(6) Some plurals are formed quite differently from those discussed above. For example:

child	children	ox	oxen	tooth	teeth
mouse	mice				

Some words derived from Latin or Greek keep their original plural endings. For example:

axis	axes	phenomenon	phenomena	radius	radii

Affixation

A thorough study should be made of the significance of roots, prefixes and suffixes. This helps with the expansion of vocabulary and has a vital bearing on spelling. To take a simple example, it helps to eradicate the mis-spelling of a number of common words like *dis-appear, dis-appointment, dis-suade, dis-satisfied* and *dis-service*. (The hyphens have been introduced here to clarify the point.)

A prefix is a small particle which is placed before the root word; a suffix is attached to the end of the root word, as in the following examples:

root word	+ *suffix*	+ *prefix*
help	helpful	unhelpful
spell	spelling	mis-spelling
appoint	appointment	disappointment
consider	considerable	inconsiderable
regular	regularly	irregularly

Sometimes the form of the prefix changes because of the attraction of the beginning consonant of the root word – the changed form being easier to say. Here are examples of how the prefix *in* can change:

religious *ir*religious   legible *il*legible   moral *im*moral.

Similarly the prefix *ob* changes to '*op*portune'; and to '*oc*casion'.

The prefix *ad* changes to '*ac*complish'; and to '*ap*plaud'.

The prefix *con* changes to '*col*laborate'; and to '*cor*rection'.

Below we give lists of (1) the more common Latin roots and examples of their English derivatives, (2) prefixes and their meanings, and (3) suffixes and their meanings.

LATIN ROOTS

Word	Meaning	Derivatives
alter	other	alteration, alternative
animus	breath, spirit	animated
arbitrium	judgement	arbitrary, arbitration
aspiro	I breathe	aspirate, aspire
audio (auditum)	I hear	audience, audition
capio (captum)	I seize	capture, captive
celero	I quicken	celerity, accelerate
clamo	I complain	clamour, exclamatory
civis	citizen	civic, civilian, civil
credo	I believe	credible, credit
cresco	I grow	crescent, increase
crux (crucis)	cross	crucial, cruciform
culpa	fault, blame	culpable, exculpate
curro (cursum)	I run	course, current, cursive
debeo (debitum)	I owe	debt, debit
dextra	right-handed	dexterity
dico (dictum)	I say, I speak	diction, dictation
duco (ductum)	I lead, I guide	duct, ductile
duro	I last, make hard	durable, duration
erro (erratum)	I wander	error, errant, aberration
famis	hunger	famine, famished
fero	I carry	transfer, ferry, infer
flecto (flexum)	I bend	flexible, inflect, reflect
flos (floris)	flower	florist, floral
frater	brother	fraternal, fratricide

frigus	cold	frigid, refrigerator
gradus	step	gradual, graded, gradient
gratus	kind, thankful	grateful, gratitude
gravis	heavy	gravity, grave
hortatio	encouragement	exhort, exhortation
hospes	guest, visitor	hospitality, hospice
incendo	I set fire to	incendiary, incense
integer	whole, entire	integrity, integral
judico	I judge	judicial, judgement
jungo (junctum)	I join	junction, juncture
lego (lectum)	I collect, I choose	collect, select
littera	letter	literate, literal
locus	place	location, locality
loquor (locutum)	I speak	loquacious, elocution
lumen	light	luminous, luminary
magister	master	magistrate, magisterial
manus	hand	manual, manuscript
mitto (missum)	I send	remit, mission
mollis	soft, tender	mollify, emollient
muto	I change	mutation, commute, immutable
narro	I tell, I relate	narrate, narrative
nox (noctis)	night	nocturnal, nocturne
nuntio	I announce	announce, announcement
opera	task	operate, operatic
oro	I pray, I speak	oratorio, oration
pater	father	patrimony, patronise
pax (pacis)	peace	pacifist, pacify
pes (pedis)	foot	pedal, pedestrian
plumbum	lead	plumber, plumb-line
poena	punishment	penalty, penal
pono (positum)	I place	position, deposit
potens	powerful	potent, potential
puer	boy	puerile, puerility
puto	I think, estimate	impute, putative
radix	root	radical, eradicate, radish

rogo	I ask	interrogate, rogation, surrogate
rumpo (ruptum)	I break, interrupt	rupture, interruption
scribo (scriptum)	I write	scripture, script, transcribe
sedeo (sessum)	I sit	sedentary, session
siccus	dry	desiccated
solus	alone	solitary, solo, soliloquy
solvo (solutum)	I loosen, explain	solution, solvent
specio (spectum)	I see, regard	spectacle, inspection
stringo (strictum)	I draw tight	stringent, strict, string
tango (tactum)	I touch	tactile, contact, tangent
teneo (tentum)	I hold	tenacious, tentacle, tenant
traho (tractum)	I draw, drag	traction, tractor, detract
verto	I turn	subvert, revert, pervert
video (visum)	I see	evident, visible, visual
vinco (victum)	I conquer	victory, convince, conviction

PREFIXES

The majority of these prefixes are derived from Latin, but a few such as *auto-, bio-, dia-* and *hemi-* are from Greek.

Prefix	Meaning	Examples
a-	on, out, up	arise
ab-	away from	abstract, abstention
ad-	to	advance, admire
amphi-	both kinds	amphibious
	around	amphitheatre
an-	not	anarchy
ante-	before	antecedent, ante-room
anti-	against	anti-aircraft, antithesis
arch-	chief	archbishop
auto-	self	automatic, autograph
bi-	having two	bicycle, bifurcate
bio-	life	biology, biography
circum-	around	circumference, circumscribe
com-	with	compact, compose
con-	with	contain, convene
contra-	against	contradict, contravene
de-	down, from	demote, depend
dia-	through	diagram, diameter

dis-	apart	dissociate, disappear
ex-	out of, from	expatriate, expose
hemi-	half	hemisphere
inter-	between	international, internal
mal-	bad	maladjusted, malformed
mis-	wrongly	misunderstood, misadventure
non-	not	non-conformist, nonsense
ob-	against	obnoxious, obloquy, objection
per-	through	persuade, perennial
post-	after	postpone, post-date
pre-	before	pre-eminent, precede, pre-empt
pro-	for, on behalf of	prologue, proclaim
re-	back	reclaim, recover, refrigerator
sub-	below	submarine, subway, subsidence
super-	above	superstar, superlative
trans-	across	transfer, transport, transmute
un-	not	undress, unacceptable
vice-	in place of	viceroy, vice-captain

SUFFIXES

Suffixes usually change the part of speech of the original word or root. They do this in various ways as these examples show:

(1) The suffix can indicate a 'doer': doct*or*; bak*er*; carpent*er*.

(2) The suffix can create an adjectival form: leg*al*; cordi*al*; wood*en*; artist*ic*; delight*ful*.

(3) The suffix can form an abstract noun: just*ice*; hom*age*; arrog*ance*.

(4) The suffix can indicate an adverbial form: slow*ly*; rough*ly*.

Suffix	*Examples*
-able, -ible, -uble	returnable, memorable, flexible, terrible, soluble
-age	marriage, suffrage, pilotage
-al, -ial	legal, regal, circumstantial
-an, -en, -ain	artisan, Italian, warden, certain
-ant, -ent	dependant, student, innocent
-ard	drunkard, steward, wizard, coward
-ary	secretary, antiquary, lapidary
-ate	accurate, desolate, mandate
-craft	handicraft, bookcraft, statecraft
-dom	freedom, kingdom, random
-er, -eer	baker, painter, engineer, profiteer

-ance, -ence	dominance, reverence, diffidence
-er, -or	waiter, porter, doctor, governor
-ery	brewery, cutlery, distillery
-ess	countess, duchess, actress
-et, -ette	coronet, signet, statuette
-fast	steadfast
-fold	manifold, fourfold
-ful	dutiful, eventful, doubtful
-hood	childhood, liklihood, manhood
-ian	magician, Christian
-ic	artistic, fabric, rubric
-ier	soldier, farrier, terrier
-ing	living, running, spending
-ion	religion, creation, indignation
-ise, -ize	advertise, disguise, summarise
-ish	childish, establish, knavish
-ism	criticism, witticism
-ist	royalist, chemist, artist
-ive	creative, positive, restive
-less	blameless, childless
-ly	manly, wickedly, softly
-ment	appointment, detriment
-ness	likeness, darkness
-ous	devious, perilous, nervous
-ry	bakery, surgery
-ship	discipleship, headship, friendship
-tude	solitude, amplitude, multitude
-ty	cruelty, dignity, brevity
-wise	clockwise, otherwise, crosswise
-y	cheeky, saucy, needy, hairy

Exercises

1. Give two examples, in each case, of English words derived from the following roots. Even if you have not studied Latin this is not a difficult exercise. For example: *equus* (a horse): equestrian, equine.

(1)	*alter*	(other)	(8) *curro*	(I run)
(2)	*arbitrium*	(judgment)	(9) *duco*	(I lead)
(3)	*aspiro*	(I breathe)	(10) *erro*	(I wander)
(4)	*capio*	(I take)	(11) *fero*	(I carry)
(5)	*civis*	(citizen)	(12) *flecto*	(I bend)
(6)	*cogito*	(I think)	(13) *gradus*	(step)
(7)	*credo*	(I believe)	(14) *impero*	(I command)

(15) *jacio*	(I throw)	(22) *pello*	(I drive)
(16) *lego*	(I collect)	(23) *pono*	(I place)
(17) *loquor*	(I speak)	(24) *rota*	(wheel)
(18) *lumen*	(light)	(25) *scribo*	(I write)
(19) *manus*	(hand)	(26) *specio*	(I see)
(20) *mitto*	(I send)	(27) *voco*	(I call)
(21) *muto*	(I change)	(28) *volvo*	(I roll)

2. By the use of a suffix, change each of the following nouns into an adjective:

(a) sister, (b) quarrel, (c) fame, (d) bother, (e) respect, (f) revenge, (g) hill, (h) gold, (i) part, (j) plenty

3. Give the meaning of the prefix in each of the following words:

(a) *ad*vent, (b) *contra*dict, (c) *juxta*pose, (d) *trans*atlantic, (e) *un*kind, (f) *ante*room, (g) *inter*vene, (h) *bene*volent, (i) *hemi*sphere, (j) *su*spend

Word lists

Students will find it very helpful to build up word lists relating to the various subjects they may be studying. This will help to eliminate many errors in spelling, and will also be useful for revision. It should be borne in mind that nothing irritates examiners more than to come across spelling errors of words that the student has seen in print and has used time and time again in the course of his studies. Human nature being what it is, an irritated examiner is usually an unsympathetic examiner. To give yourself the best chance in an examination, therefore, it is worth while giving careful attention to spelling.

Below we give two typical word lists that apply to (*a*) general or combined science, and (*b*) geography. They are meant to be suggestive rather than exhaustive.

GENERAL OR COMBINED SCIENCE

The following list of words covers most of the technical terms used in the teaching of general science, combined science or environmental science up to the first public examination – C.S.E. or G.C.E. Ordinary level, or any amalgamation of these examinations in the future. The list excludes many of the terms employed in the more detailed study of chemistry, physics and the biological sciences when treated as separate examination subjects. Students who are interested in dictionary definitions rather than a spelling approach should consult *An Elementary Scientific and Technical Dictionary* by W. E. Flood and M. West, published by Longman, London, revised edition, 1962. Our concern here is with spelling, and the list is based on current classroom practice, which itself is largely determined by the syllabuses of the various examination boards.

abdomen	allotropic	antenna
absorb	alternating	antimony
absorption	ammonia	apparatus
acceleration	amoeba	aquatic
acid	amorphous	asexual
adrenalin	ampere	atmosphere
advantage	amplify	atom
aerated	anaerobic	attraction
aerobic	analysis	autoclave
alcohol	aneroid	axle
alimentary	anhydrous	
alkali	anode	bacteria

barometer
battery
beaker
behaviour
benzene
biennial
bimetallic
bismuth
bleach
bowel
bunsen
burette
butterfly

calcium
calibrate
callipers
candle
capacitance
capillary
carbohydrate
carbon
carboniferous
carnivorous
catalyst
caterpillar
cathode
cavity
cellular
Centrigrade
characteristic
charcoal
chemistry
chlorine
chlorophyll
chromatic
chromosome
chrysalis
ciliary
circuit
circulation

circumference
clavicle
colloidal
combustion
component
compound
concave
concentrated
condenser
conductor
conifer
conservation
contract
convection
converging
convex
cornea
corpuscle
cotyledon
crank
crystal
crystallise
cube
current
cycle
cylinder

decibel
deciduous
decimal
degree
deliquescent
density
deposit
diagonal
diffraction
diffusion
digestion
dilute
diminished
diploid

direct
distil
distillation
diverging
drug
duodenum
dye
dynamo

effervescent
efficiency
efflorescence
elasticity
electricity
electrode
electrolysis
electron
electrostatics
element
embryo
emulsify
emulsion
endocrine
enzyme
equation
equivalent
evaporate
evergreen
expand
extract

Fahrenheit
femur
ferment
ferrous
fertilise
fibre
filament
flask
flotation
fluorescent

foetus
forceps
formula
fossil
fractional
frequency
friction
fulcrum
function
fungus
funnel
fusion

gamete
gaseous
gauge
gauze
gear
gene
generate
genetic
genotype
germinate
gland
glycerol
gramme
graph
gravity

haemoglobin
haemophilia
halogen
haploid
harmonic
helium
herbivorous
heredity
hermaphrodite
homogeneous
hormone
humerus

humidity
humus
hydra
hydrated
hydraulic
hydrocarbon
hydrochloric
hydrogen
hydrolysis
hydrometer
hygiene
hygroscopic
hypothesis

induction
inertia
infectious
inflorescence
inhale
inject
insoluble
insulate
insulin
integrated
interference
iodine
ion
isomer
isotype

joule

kidney
kinetic

labium
laboratory
lamina
larva
lava
lens

liquefy
liquid
litmus
liver

magnesium
magnetism
magnify
mammal
mandible
manganese
manometer
mass
mathematical
maxilla
mechanical
meiosis
membrane
meniscus
mercury
metre
mica
micropyle
microscope
mineral
mitosis
molecule
momentum
mould
multicellular
muscle

negative
neon
nervous
neutral
neutron
newton
nitrogen
non-aqueous
nucleus

nutrition
nymph

orbit
organic
organism
osmosis
ovule
oxide
oxidation
oxidise
oxygen

pancreas
parabolic
paraffin
parallel
parasite
particle
pendulum
perennial
period
permeate
perspiration
petroleum
phenomenon
phenotype
phosphorus
photosynthesis
pipette
pistil
piston
pituitary
pivot
placenta
planet
platelet
platinum
plumule
polarised
polarity

pollinate
positive
potassium
potential
power
precipitate
pressure
prism
prismatic
proboscis
propagation
propeller
property
protein
proton
pulley
pupa

qualitative
quantitative
quinine

radiation
radicle
radioactive
radium
radius
ratio
receptor
reflection
reflex
refraction
repulsion
resin
resistance
respiration
retina
rheostat

salt
saturated

sclerotic
secrete
sedimentary
sepal
septic
sinusoidal
siphon
skeleton
skull
soda
sodium
solenoid
solidify
soluble
solution
solvent
specific
spectrum
sphincter
sphygmomanometer
spine
spirogyra
spore
stamen
sterilise
sternum
stigma
stimulus
stomach
storage
structure
sulphur
synthetic
syringe
system

tadpole
technical
telescope
temperature
tendril

tension	ultraviolet	velocity
testa	umbilical	vertebrate
thermal	uranium	virus
thermometer	urine	vitamin
thermostat		volatile
thyroid	vacuole	volt
tibia	vacuum	volume
tissue	valency	
trachea	valve	weight
translucent	vaporisation	
transparent	vapour	yeast
transpiration	vegetable	
	vegetative	zinc
ulna	vein	zygote

GEOGRAPHY

In addition to the list suggested below, the student should build up a list of proper names (continents, countries, towns, rivers, mountains and so on) according to the regions being studied.

agriculture	erosion	magnetic
amenities	estuary	metamorphic
anemometer		migration
anticyclone	faulting	morphology
arable	fisheries	
arctic	folding	oblique
	forestry	ocean
barometer		ordnance
	global	
compass	gradient	pastoral
conurbation	Greenwich	physical
current		population
	horizon	
deposition		rain-gauge
depression	igneous	relief
distribution	intensive	resources
	intervisibility	rock-cleavage
economic		rural
energy	latitude	
environment	lithosphere	salinity
equator	longitude	sedimentary

sphere	temperate	variation
statistics	thermometer	vegetation
strike		
survey	urbanisation	weathering

FIVE HUNDRED DIFFICULT SPELLINGS

Most English-speaking countries have carried out research to find out the words whose spelling cause difficulty and there is a large measure of agreement on this. The following words are known to cause difficulty. They should be frequently looked at, memorised and used in meaningful contexts as often as possible. Sometimes the words can be helpfully linked with spelling rules. Properly organised dictation practice and various word quiz-games can also help.

absence	anoint	bureau
abyss	antecedent	
accelerate	apologise	campaign
acceptable	appalling	carburettor
access	applause	career
accessories	assassination	carefully
accident	athlete	carriage
accidentally	authorise	caterpillar
accommodation	autumnal	cautionary
accumulation	auxiliary	cease
accuracy	awkward	celerity
achievement		cemetery
acknowledgement	beautiful	censure
acquaintance	believing	ceremony
acquire	beneficial	changeable
acre	benefited	chaos
adequate	benign	character
advisable	benignant	chasm
aerial	bequeath	chauffeur
aerodrome	bicycle	chimney
aeroplane	bisect	chocolate
aircraft	blancmange	choice
aisle	boatswain	choose
alleged	bookkeeper	clerk
alleviate	bouquet	clientele
amount	brochure	colleague
analysis	bulletin	college

colossal
column
committee
complementary
complimentary
concede
concession
conscience
conscientious
concrete
contemporary
correspondence
corroborate
council (*n*)
counsel (*v*)
courtesy
creative
criticism
cushion
cycle

dearth
decision
deficient
depreciation
desirable
desperate
despise
dialogue
diaphragm
difference
dinghy
diphtheria
diphthong
disappeared
disappointment
disciple
discipline
dissatisfied
doctor
doctrine

drought
dungaree
dungeon

earache
eccentric
eclipse
efficient
eligible
embarrass
eminent
endeavour
enforceable
enormous
enthusiasm
equipped
equitable
equivalent
erroneous
especially
exaggerate
exceed
excellent
exceptionally
excerpt
excessive
exchangeable
exhaustive
experience
experimentally
extraordinary
extremely

failure
familiar
famine
feasible
feature
February
feudalism
fierce

fiery
financial
finesse
fission
fluidity
foible
forcible
foreign
forfeit
formerly
forty
fourth
freight
frightened
frigidity
frontier
fruit
fruitful
fugue
fulfil
furniture
fuselage
futile

gaol
gaudy
gauge
gauze
genuine
gesture
geyser
giraffe
gorgeous
government
grievance
grotesque
group
guarantee
guerrilla
guidance
guide

handicap
handsome
harbour
haughty
headache
health
hearth
heaven
heifer
hoarse
homage
horrified
humane
humorous
humour
 (U.S. humor)
hurried
hyphen

ignoble
illegible
illiterate
illuminate
immediately
immigration
imminent
immune
inadequate
inaugurate
indefinite
independent
indict
indispensable
inducement
ineligible
inevitably
inexplicable
infectious
ingenious
initiate
innocence

inoculate
inquisitive
insatiable
insurance
intellect
intelligible
intercede
intercession
interruption
intricate
invariable
irrelevant
isosceles
isthmus

jealous
jeopardise
Jesuit
jewel
jeweller
jocular
journal
journey
jubilation
judgement
 (or judgment)
judicial
judicious
jurisprudence
justifiable
justified
juvenile
juxtaposition

khaki
kleptomania
knack
knead
knight
knock
knot

knowledge
knowledgeable

label
laboratory
laborious
labour
 (U.S. labor)
lacquer
language
laughter
launch
league
learn
legible
leisure
length
lettuce
liable
licence
license
lieutenant
lightning
linguist
liquid
liquor
literary
luncheon

machine
machinery
maintain
maintenance
manageable
manoeuvre
medical
medicine
mediocre
mercantile
merchandise
microphone

miniature
miscellaneous
mischief
mischievous
misdemeanour
mis-spell
monastery
mortgage
moustache
mysterious
mystery

naturally
necessary
necessity
negligible
neighbour
  (U.S. neighbor)
nephew
nervous
notorious
nuclear

obsolete
obvious
occasionally
offered
official
omission
omitted
onerous
opportunity
optimist
orchestra
original
overhaul
overrate

pamphlet
papacy
paraffin

parallel
paralyse
parliament
particular
pavilion
perennial
permissible
permitting
pernicious
persevere
persistent
personal
personnel
pharmacist
philosophy
physician
physics
polytechnic
possessive
precedent
predecessor
preferable
preferred
preliminary
prerogative
prescription
prevalence
prevalent
privacy
prodigal
prodigious
prodigy
professor
profited
progeny
propaganda
prophecy (*n*)
prophesy (*v*)
propriety
psalm
psychic

psychology

quadrilateral
quadruped
quadruplets
quarantine
quartz
quay
querulous
questionnaire
quixotic

radiance
receptacle
recognise
reconciliation
reconnaissance
referee
reference
referred
regrettably
reiterate
relief
religious
reminiscence
renaissance
repertoire
repertory
representative
requisition
resurrect
reticence
rhetoric

sacrilegious
salutary
sarcasm
satellite
saturate
scarcity
scenery

schedule
science
secondary
secrecy
secretary
sedition
seize
sensitive
separate
sergeant
serviceable
shepherd
significant
silhouette
sincere
sinecure
skeleton
soliloquy
soluble
solution
sophisticated
souvenir
sovereignty
specialist
specimen
spontaneity
stationary
  (not moving)
stationery
  (writing material)
stoicism
strenuous
subsistence
subterranean
successful
succession
suicide
superficial
supersede

supplement
supremacy
surgery
surveillance
syllogism
symmetrical
symphony
synopsis
synthesis
syphon
system
systematic

tactical
tantalise
tautology
technical
technique
technology
temperament
temporary
temporarily
tessellated
thoroughly
threatening
thyroid
titillate
titivate
tobacconist
tragedy
tragical
transcendental
transfer
transferable
treachery
treason
treasury
troubadour
truly

tunnel
tunnelling
turquoise
twelfth
typical

ubiquitous
unconscionable
unilateral
utilitarianism

vacation
vaccination
vacillate
vague
vassal
vehicle
vendetta
veneer
veterinary
vicious
vitreous
viviparous

weight
wreckage
wrestle
writhe

yeast
yeoman
yield

zealot
zenith
zephyr
zest
zodiac
zoological

American spelling

Throughout the world many English Language schools have been established by Americans, and American books, newspapers and magazines have a worldwide circulation. Consequently students of English everywhere will meet American spelling. Below we list some examples of the differences that can occur.

EXAMPLES

	British	*American*
ae is usually replaced by *e*	haemoglobin	hemoglobin
	haemorrhage	hemorrhage
	aegis	egis
	aesthetic	esthetic
oe is usually replaced by *e*	foetus	fetus
	manoeuvre	maneuver
	oesophagus	esophagus
	phoenix	phenix
-our is usually replaced by *-or*	colour	color
	honour	honor
	humour	humor
	labour	labor
	odour	odor
	rumour	rumor
	vigour	vigor
	neighbour	neighbor
l is often replaced by *ll*	enrol	enroll
	enthral	enthrall
	enrolment	enrollment
	fulfil	fulfill
	wilful	willful
	instalment	installment
	fulfilment	fulfillment
	skilful	skillful
	instil	instill
-mme is replaced by *-m*	programme	program
-ogue is often replaced by *-og*	catalogue	catalog
	analogue	analog
-re is replaced by *-er*	centre	center
	metre	meter
	theatre	theater

c in '-ence' is replaced by s	defence	defense
	offence	offense
	pretence	pretense
c in '-ice' is replaced by s	practice (n.)	practise (n.)
'-nce' is replaced by s	licence (n.)	license (n.)
'-cy' is replaced by s	prophecy (n.)	prophesy (n.)
the -ise ending is usually -ize	improvise	improvize
(see below)		

NOTE: Nowadays the *Oxford English Dictionary, the Encyclopedia Britannica, The Times* and the Cambridge University Press treat the suffix -ize as an accepted form. The Americans have long settled for -ize. In Britain, however, a number of quite important words must take the -ise ending, for example:

advertise	demise	enterprise	precise
chastise	despise	exercise	supervise
comprise	disguise	improvise	surmise
compromise	enfranchise	incise	surprise

Exercises

1. Give the plural of:

potato	goose	monkey	sister-in-law
fly	echo	day	studio
valley	chief	child	leaf
calf	mouse	court martial	manservant
solo	axis	stimulus	daisy
wife	shelf	calf	journey

2. Add suffixes to each of the following:

advance	achieve	service	true
agree	manage	devote	courage
care	active	crime	verb
art	fast	holy	will

3. Form words ending in '-ed' or '-ing' from the following:

slip	split	float	marry
bat	profit	marshal	hurry
coach	prevail	defy	dry
teem	seed	journey	sigh
eat	station	lose	whip

4. Add suffixes to the following nouns to make, in each case, (a) an adjective, (b) an adverb. *Example*: care (n): careful (*adj*); carefully (*adv*).

might	honour	play	minimum
hope	energy	drama	deceit
fury	fraction		

5. Add '-able' or -ible' to form the correct spelling of the following. Example: not. . . notable   poss. . . possible

explic . . .	depend . . .	companion . . .	inflamm . . .
aud . . .	ten . . .	cred . . .	feas . . .
manage . . .	gull . . .	incur . . .	understand . . .
permiss . . .	applic . . .	detest . . .	

6. Add prefixes to form the negatives of the following. Example: audible   inaudible

satisfied	similar	successful	official
regular	legible	determinate	orthodox

Part 5

Vocabulary

Synonyms, antonyms and homophones

Synonyms

Synonyms are words of approximately the same meaning; for example:

quickly   speedily   reinforced   strengthened

The following list of synonyms will provide you with a set of words of associated meaning which may, in appropriate circumstances, be very useful.

abnormal	unusual, exceptional, odd, peculiar
abridge	shorten, curtail, condense
abundant	plentiful, copious, ample
accumulate	collect, acquire, get together, build up
acquiesce	agree, assent, consent, concur
amazement	surprise, astonishment, bewilderment
arduous	hard, difficult, strenuous
bold	brave, courageous, confident, enterprising
brief	short, concise, limited
bright	shining, brilliant, gleaming, dazzling
brusque	blunt, off-hand, sharp
cautious	careful, circumspect, heedful
competent	qualified, able, effective
conspicuous	outstanding, obvious, striking
covetous	envious, greedy
decay	rot, decompose, decline
deceive	cheat, mislead, misrepresent, lie
depose	remove, unseat, demote
detest	hate, loathe, abominate
discord	strife, quarrel, disagreement
efficient	competent, effective, capable
eminent	distinguished, notable, outstanding
exquisite	delicate, fine, keen (of pleasure)
famous	notable, noted, renowned, eminent
fascinating	captivating, alluring, absorbing, irresistible
festive	joyous, jovial, happy

generous	free, liberal, open-handed, copious
genial	friendly, warm, kindly
genuine	authentic, true, reputed, warranted
hazardous	dangerous, risky, reckless
hideous	repulsive, frightening, revolting
humble	lowly, modest
impudent	cheeky, pert, shameless
inception	start, beginning
irate	angry, annoyed, furious
indelicate	tactless, immodest, coarse
jubilant	joyful, delighted
just	honest, upright, fair
knavery	dishonesty, roguery, wickedness
lament	sorrow, grief, elegy
languid	feeble, faint, drooping
liberal	generous, free, unprejudiced
manifest	show, demonstrate, reveal
meagre	scarce, thin, scanty, insufficient
miniature	small, diminutive, tiny
needy	poor, necessitous, wanting
normal	usual, regular, ordinary
notable	important, famous, known
odium	hate, dislike, loathing
option	choice, preference
potent	strong, powerful, cogent, influential
precise	exact, definite, scrupulous
prudent	wise, careful, discreet
quench	slake (thirst), extinguish, stifle
querulous	complaining, peevish, dissatisfied
recompense	reward, requite, compensate
refresh	re-animate, re-invigorate, restore
refuge	shelter, haven
slender	thin, slim, scanty
solitary	single, alone, isolated
staid	quiet, sober, withdrawn
talented	gifted, clever, brilliant
urge	exhort, press, entreat
vivacious	lively, bright, cheerful
waver	vacillate, hesitate, change (opinion)
wicked	evil, wrong, devilish
wretched	unhappy, miserable, poor

Antonyms

Antonyms are words of approximately the opposite meaning; for example:

quick   slow   dead   alive   hurry   delay

These are less important than synonyms, for we must always have the latter at our fingertips when striving to achieve variety in our written work. It is interesting, however, to see how they may be formed, and familiarity with them assists us to expand our vocabulary.

We have already seen how prefixes can modify the meanings of words. Here we see how different prefixes can produce words of opposite meaning:

regular	irregular	polite	impolite
certain	uncertain	ascent	descent
soluble	insoluble	external	internal
perfect	imperfect	increase	decrease
order	disorder	inside	outside

Many antonyms, however, are completely different words:

alive	dead	hard	soft
height	depth	rough	smooth
rich	poor	love	hate
retire	advance	generous	miserly
question	answer	senior	junior

It is well to remember that no two words are absolutely identical or opposite in meaning. Every word has subtle overtones and associations, and for this reason there can never be any perfect synonyms or antonyms.

The classic reference book on synonyms and antonyms is the well-known *Thesaurus of English Words and Phrases*, originally by Peter Roget, revised by Susan M. Lloyd and published by Longman. There are also many useful Crossword Dictionaries that serve a similar purpose.

Homophones

Homophones are words like *boy* and *buoy* that sound alike but have different meanings. Some homophones cause confusion and therefore need to be looked at carefully – and remembered. Two common examples are:

principal   principle   stationary   stationery

Here is a fairly representative list of homophones:

aisle	isle	ascent	assent
aloud	allowed	beach	beech

board	bored	pale	pail
boy	buoy	pause	paws
canon	cannon	pier	peer
cereal	serial	plane	plain
chord	cord	principal	principle
course	coarse	raise	raze
cymbal	symbol	rein	rain
draft	draught	rite	right
formally	formerly	roll	role
gage	gauge	sew	sow
hair	hare	site	sight
hall	haul	stair	stare
holy	wholly	stake	steak
horse	hoarse	stationary	stationery
its	it's	tale	tail
kernel	colonel	there	their
leak	leek	waist	waste
lesson	lessen	waive	wave
maize	maze	weather	whether
mayor	mare	whose	who's
moor	more	vain	vane
muse	mews	yoke	yolk

Exercises

1. Replace the italicised words with suitable synonyms:

(a) His *reverie* was suddenly disturbed.
(b) He was a man of remarkable *meekness*.
(c) I want your full *acquiescence* in the matter.
(d) It was an obvious *falsehood*.
(e) I shall *request* a return match; our opponents promised this.
(f) He *disclaimed* any knowledge of the theft.
(g) He *studiously* avoided any contact with his opponent.
(h) His explanation was very *lucid*.
(i) The *import* of his statement was not clear.
(j) He *arranged* the whole outing very competently.

2. Suggest two synonyms for each of the following words:

advocate	convey	eccentric	heave
banish	dazed	eclipse	homage
batter	delusion	elevate	hurt
catastrophe	detest	flee	ignite
comprehend	devastate	forecast	impulsive

juvenile	nasty	prestige	rational
laconic	opponent	prevail	rectify
laughable	overthrow	quicken	renounce
manufacture	parade	raise	renowned
morbid	particular	ramble	stately

3. Each of the following questions starts with a pair of synonyms. Place the appropriate synonyms in the sentence below. This exercise shows you that synonyms are not necessarily interchangeable; it all depends upon the context.

(a) *honest*   *just*

...... politicians try to achieve a ...... peace.

(b) *old*   *antique*

The ...... furniture suited the ...... house.

(c) *careful*   *prudent*

A ...... man is ...... with the money.

(d) *modern*   *new*

In the ...... town there was some very ...... architecture.

(e) *cure*   *remedy*

The sprinter found a ...... that was a certain ......

(f) *shining*   *bright*

It was a ...... day and the sun was always ......

4. Re-arrange these sets of five synonyms in order of 'strength'. For example:

safe, secure, impregnable, protected, invulnerable

Answer: safe, protected, secure, invulnerable, impregnable

(a) discourteous, ill-mannered, churlish, abusive, pert
(b) magnificent, stately, gorgeous, imposing, majestic
(c) dangerous, risky, hazardous, precarious, perilous
(d) generous, bountiful, free, liberal, unselfish
(e) laconic, abridged, short, brief, concise
(f) weak, feeble, delicate, frail, infirm
(g) hideous, grotesque, ugly, repulsive, unsightly
(h) perplexed, confused, nonplussed, puzzled, baffled
(i) cordial, friendly, hospitable, civil, courteous
(j) energetic, active, industrious, lively, spirited

5. Suggest antonyms for the following words:

clever	wealth	beautiful	luxurious
sound	slovenly	accept	obstinate
front	indubitable	busy	derelict
deny	polite	intelligent	cantankerous
dejected	quiet	plentiful	exemption
shallow	innocent	difficult	nullify

6. Choose the correct word:

   (a) This ...... of glass is broken. (pain; pane)
   (b) ...... house is this? (Who's; whose)
   (c) She was ...... introduced at the dinner. (formerly; formally)
   (d) To me it is a matter of ...... (principal; principle)
   (e) The boys had no idea ...... they ...... (were; where)
   (f) The building ...... was very muddy. (sight; site)
   (g) It will ...... his chance of being caught. (lessen; lesson)
   (h) We usually ...... seeds in the spring. (sew; sow)
   (i) ...... not, want not. (waist; waste)
   (j) He ordered an underdone ...... (steak; stake)

7. Write short sentences using the following words correctly:

   (a) stationary, (b) chord, (c) role, (d) assent, (e) cannon, (f) peer, (g) board, (h) coarse, (i) yoke, (j) serial

8. Write short sentences using the following pairs of words correctly:

(a) vein	(c) muse	(e) draught	(g) stair	(i) its
(b) vane	(d) mews	(f) draft	(h) stare	(j) it's

Nouns of assembly

An interesting verbal curiosity is the following list of special collective nouns, called 'nouns of assembly'. They are a useful addition to the student's vocabulary, but should be employed sparingly since many of them are rarely used, even by native speakers of English.

a herd of antelope
a shrewdness of apes
a pace or herd of asses
a cete of badgers
a sleuth (or sloth) of bears
a swarm or grist of bees
a flock or flight of birds
a sedge or siege of bitterns
a sounder of boars
a brace or leash of bucks
a herd of buffaloes
a drove or herd of cattle
a brood of chickens
a chattering of choughs
a covert of coots
a murder of crows
a litter of cubs
a herd of deer
a paddling of ducks (*in the water*)
a team of ducks (*in flight*)
a gang of elk
a fesnyng of ferrets
a shoal, draught or haul of fishes
a swarm of flies
a skulk of foxes
a gaggle of geese (*on ground*)
a skein of geese (*in flight*)
a herd or tribe of goats
a charm of goldfinches
a covey of grouse
a colony of gulls (*breeding*)
a down or husk of hares
a cast of hawks
a brood of hens
a sedge or siege of herons

a shoal of herrings
a pack or mute of hounds
a swarm of insects
a troop of kangaroos
a kindle of kittens
an exaltation of larks
a leap of leopards
a pride of lions
a stud of mares
a labour of moles
a troop of monkeys
a barren of mules
a watch of nightingales
a yoke, drove or team of oxen
a covey of partridges
a muster of peacocks
a nye or nide of pheasants
a flock or flight of pigeons
a wing or congregation of plovers
a school of porpoises
a litter of pups
a bevy of quails
a nest of rabbits
a building or clamour of rooks
a herd or pod of seals
a flock of sheep
a host of sparrows
a murmuration of starlings
a flight of swallows
a herd or bevy of swans
a sounder or drift of swine
a school or pod of whales
a pod of whiting
a pack, rout or herd of wolves
a fall of woodcock

Phils, phobias, ologies and isms

Here are some interesting and unusual words. Many of them originate in the fields of medicine and science – these are chiefly the *phobias, ologies* and *isms* – but some of the most recent are the coinages of witty journalists. Many of these very new words do not yet appear in dictionaries, but will gradually appear in Appendices and Supplements. A growing number of medical terms tend to become part of popular usage, for example, 'geriatric', 'syndrome', 'dipsomania' 'dyslexia', 'allergic' and 'claustrophobia'. You will observe the importance of roots, prefixes and suffixes in this field of word formation.

-phile or -phily:

acrophile	a lover of mountains
anglophile	a lover of England and/or the English
cartophily	the collecting of cigarette cards
cumyxaphily	the collecting of match-boxes
discophily	the collecting of gramophone records
hippophile	a lover of horses
peridromophily	the collecting of bus and railway tickets
stegophily	a love of climbing buildings

-ology

anemology	the science of the winds
arachnology	the study of spiders
campanology	the study of bells and bell-ringing
conchology	the science of shells
coprology	obscenity in art and literature
deltiology	the collecting of picture post-cards
dendrochronology	the dating by growth of annual rings in trees
eschatology	the doctrine of death and after-life
gerontology	the study of old age
hagiology	the study of the saints
herpetology	the study of reptiles
nelittology	the study of bees
numismatology	the collecting of coins
orology	the study of mountains
pneumatology	the study of spiritual beings or phenomena
psephology	the scientific study of political elections
scatology	the study of pornographic literature
speleology	the study of caves
tegestology	the collecting and study of beer mats
vulcanology	the study of volcanoes

-phobia:

agoraphobia	fear of open spaces
amaxophobia	an abnormal fear of riding in vehicles
anglophobia	hatred of England and the English
aphephobia	an abnormal fear of being touched
astraphobia	a morbid fear of lightning
automysophobia	an abnormal fear of being dirty
brontophobia	a morbid fear of thunder
cenophobia	a morbid fear of open spaces
claustrophobia	fear of enclosed spaces
cynophobia	fear of dogs
doraphobia	an abnormal fear of animal skins
gallophobia	hatred of France and the French
hypsophobia	fear of heights
melissophobia	fear of bees
osmophobia	an abnormal fear of odours
taphophobia	fear of being buried alive
xenophobia	fear of foreigners

-ism:

albinism	the state of being an albino, lacking normal pigmentation – having white hair and pink eyes
aneurism	a disease of the arteries
totalitarianism	one-party state or government

-ist:

aerophilatelist	one who collects air-mail stamps
misogynist	one who hates women
philanthropist	one who loves mankind

-mania:

anthomania	a great love of flowers
bibliokleptomania	a mental aberration leading to the stealing of books
dipsomania	the compulsion to drink alcohol
pyromania	the compulsion to start fires

OTHERS:

acronym	a word made up of the initials of a title: e.g. NATO; SALT; UNESCO
aesthetics	relating to the study or appreciation of beauty

aficionado	a keen follower of a sport, specially of bullfighting in Spain
alopecia	baldness
amnesia	loss of memory
anorexia	loss of apetite
capnomancy	divination from smoke
cartomancy	divination from playing cards
cheironomy	the science of expression by means of gestures
dyslexia	word blindness
misandry	a morbid fear of men by women
phonocamptics	the study of echoes
pyrotechnics	fireworks
rhabdomancy	divination by rods (dowsing)
serendipity	an aptitude for making fortunate discoveries accidentally
syndrome	a set of symptoms

Confusing pairs of words

Some English words are somewhat similar in sound and/or spelling, though often quite different in meaning. Below is listed a selection of these pairs of words. Look them up in your dictionary where necessary so that you are quite clear about the differences. Then choose some of the pairs and write short sentences to show the meaning of each word. Note that, in an exercise of this kind, if you are asked to illustrate the use of the word 'illiterate' for example, it is not enough to write 'The boy was quite illiterate', for this does not bring out the meaning clearly. You need to add a further comment to make the meaning absolutely clear; in this case the correct answer would be, 'the boy was quite illiterate; he could neither read nor write the simplest sentences.'

accept	except	course	coarse
access	excess	deride	derive
affection	affectation	devise	device
amateur	armature	dilate	dilute
amiable	amenable	effect	affect
apposite	opposite	elude	delude
casual	causal	emminent	imminent
censure	censor	exasperate	exacerbate
complement	compliment	exercise	exorcise
conceive	concede	fertile	futile
continual	continuous	fiction	faction

gage	gauge	petition	partition
genteel	gentle	portable	potable
gourmet	gourmand	principal	principle
gracious	graceful	propagate	promulgate
humidity	humility	proceed	precede
illegible	ineligible	prophesy	prophecy
illusion	allusion	psychic	physic
imprudent	impudent	rapport	report
ingenious	ingenuous	recourse	resource
intelligible	intelligent	reflect	deflect
intimate	intimidate	resent	recent
inure	injure	reverent	reverend
judicial	judicious	sedentary	sedimentary
juggler	jugular	seller	cellar
largesse	largeness	sensual	sensuous
legible	eligible	septic	sceptic
lessen	lesson	sever	severe
metal	mettle	siege	seize
militant	militate	stationary	stationery
misery	miserly	statue	statute
mollify	modify	structure	stricture
moral	morale	symbol	cymbal
obedience	obeisance	tumultuous	tumulus
obsequies	obsequious	turpentine	turpitude
obsolete	obsolescent	uninterested	disinterested
official	officious	venal	venial
oral	aural	veracious	voracious

Foreign words and phrases

This section lists, defines and illustrates the use of foreign words and phrases that appear quite frequently in books, periodicals and newspapers. Many of the terms also crop up quite naturally in conversation and discussion. In every case the original language of the word or phrase is indicated, Latin and French being the main sources. With the decline in the teaching of languages in schools it becomes more important than ever to familiarise ourselves with the meaning and use of these words and phrases, for many of them are now an intrinsic part of English usage.

a fortiori: (*Latin*) literally, 'from yet firmer ground' or 'with stronger reason'. It is a term from logic and is used as in the following: 'The bank refused him a loan of £500; *a fortiori* he had no hope of borrowing £10,000.'

a priori: (*Latin*) literally, 'from the former'. This is another term from logic, referring to an inferential argument – a fact deduced from something antecedent or from the general to the particular. All mathematical proofs, for example, are *a priori*.

à propos: (*French*) 'to the point' or 'with reference to', as in '*A propos* our discussion yesterday, I have now decided not to invite him to our meeting.'

ad infinitum: (*Latin*) 'to infinity'. Example: 'Little fleas have smaller fleas upon their backs to bite 'em./Smaller fleas have lesser fleas, so on *ad infinitum*.'

ad nauseam: (*Latin*) 'to the point of disgust'. Example: 'I get thoroughly fed up with Tom; he goes on about politics *ad nauseam*.'

al fresco: (*Italian*) 'in the open air'. Example: 'Let's have an *al fresco* party near the river tomorrow.'

alibi: (*Latin*) literally, 'elsewhere'. The term is originally a legal one; it refers to a plea in defence that the defendant seeks to prove that he was elsewhere at the time the crime was committed.

alma mater: (*Latin*) literally, 'bounteous mother'. The term is still used by graduates in referring to the University where they studied. Example: 'John Harvard, Sir Isaac Newton, John Milton and Prince Charles have a common *alma mater* – Cambridge.'

amour propre: (*French*) 'self-love' or 'self-esteem'. Example: 'It hurt his *amour propre* to be rejected by the electorate he had served loyally for twenty-five years.'

aqua vitae: (*Latin*) literally, 'water of life', a term applied to brandy which is a well-known restorative at moments of collapse. Example: 'Quick, bring the smelling salts and some *aqua vitae*; she has fainted.'

bête noire: (*French*) literally, 'black beast', meaning metaphorically 'one's special abomination or hate'. Example: 'The Common Market was his *bête noire*; he would carry on about it for hours on end.'

billet-doux: (*French*) 'a love letter'. Example: 'Every day she found a *billet doux* from her admirer on her desk.'

blasé: (*French*) tired of pleasure; surfeited; over-sophisticated. Example: 'As a weekly commuter to New York he had become quite *blasé* about air-travel.'

bona fide: (*Latin*) in good faith, genuine. Example: 'As a *bona fide* pensioner, he applied for concessionary rail fares whenever he travelled.'

bon vivant and **bon viveur:** (*French*) meaning 'good living' and 'a good liver'; hence a gourmet or connoisseur of good food and wine. Example: 'He was a noted *bon viveur* and was famed far and wide for his love of good food.'

bourgeoisie: (*French*) the term historically denotes the social class between the gentry and the labourers and artisans; it is the solid lower middle class of merchants, shopkeepers and white-collar workers in general. Nowadays, the adjective *bourgeois* is commonly used to mean 'middle class' generally, often in a pejorative sense, as in 'His whole way of life reflects the *bourgeois* values to which he has sunk – an "executive" house, two cars, holidays in the Caribbean and his children in independent schools.'

bric-à-brac: (*French*) antiquarian or artistic odds and ends. Example: 'At the auction one room was filled with *bric-à-brac* of all shapes and sizes.'

carte blanche: (*French*) literally, 'a white paper'; hence metaphorically 'an open invitation' or 'complete permission'. Example: 'You have been appointed manager of the factory, so you have *carte blanche* to introduce whatever reforms you consider necessary.'

chacun à son goût: (*French*) 'Every man to his taste'. Example: 'When you are considering the merits of wines, it is always a case of *chacun à son goût*.'

chargé d'affaires: (*French*) a person entrusted with affairs of state abroad, frequently an acting ambassador. Example: 'The new African state has no ambassador from France at the moment, only a *chargé d'affaires*.'

contretemps: (*French*) an awkward mischance, a misunderstanding. Example: 'It was an unfortunate *contretemps* for Jim, when he phoned his girlfriend and heard the voice of her father at the other end.'

coup de grâce: (*French*) finishing stroke. Example: 'As the farmer collected the rabbits from the snares, he expertly administered the *coup de grâce*.'

cul de sac: (*French*) a blind alley, Literally, the bottom of a sack. Example: 'While fighting their way through the maze of streets, the section suddenly found itself trapped in a *cul de sac*; there was no way out.'

curriculum vitae: (*Latin*) a record of one's life history. This phrase is frequently met in making an application for a post. The employers wish to know the applicants's age, place of birth, schools, academic qualifications, experience in other jobs and so on. Often written c.v. Example: 'Candidates for the post must submit a full *curriculum vitae*.'

de facto: (*Latin*) 'in fact' or 'in reality'. This is a legal term contrasting with the parallel phrase *de jure*. In all struggles for power, the winner becomes the actual leader or ruler: he is the *de facto* leader, even if he has no legal basis for his position. Official status may follow later and the *de facto* ruler eventually becomes legally regularised – that is, *de jure*. A classic case is the independence of the American 'colonies'. At the beginning of the American War of Independence the Americans were legally rebels and traitors although *de facto* they exercised independence. A legal treaty of independence was eventually signed.

deus ex machina: (*Latin*) literally, 'the god from the machine', a term derived from Greek drama, when a complicated plot could be resolved by the unexpected appearance of a God or some key person. Example: 'In many "westerns" the U.S. cavalry arrives like a *deus ex machina* just as the Indians are about to win.'

double entendre: (*French*) having a double meaning. This term covers hints and innuendoes as well as witty puns. Shakespeare employs this device in *The Merchant of Venice*: 'So is the will of a living daughter curbed by the will of a dead father.' Example: 'Some wily politicians are masters of the *double entendre*.' Sometimes the noun form, *double entente*, is used.

dramatis personae: (*Latin*) the characters in a play. Example: 'At the theatre the programme usually lists the characters under the heading *dramatis personae*.'

ennui: (*French*) boredom, depression. Example: 'In a state of depression and *ennui*, Hamlet expresses his feelings in the words: "How weary, stale, flat and unprofitable seem to me all the uses of this world".'

entente cordiale: (*French*) a cordial and complete understanding between two sovereign powers. Example: 'After the era of de Gaulle, the traditional *entente cordiale* between France and Britain became rather strained.'

entre nous: *(French)* between us, privately. Example: 'I can get you some very good clothes at a discount, but it must be strictly *entre nous*.'

esprit de corps: *(French)* a spirit of unity and solidarity with one's comrades. Example: 'The *esprit de corps* of the soldiers was particularly notable during the Falklands War. Their courage and professional dedication were very apparent.'

ex officio: *(Latin)* by virtue of his office. The term is widely used in committee work. Example: 'Mr Macnamara is our new chairman and he will, of course, be an *ex officio* member of the two sub-committees we have just established.'

hors de combat: *(French)* literally, 'out of the fight', hence 'disabled'. Example: 'After a ferocious tackle the outside half was rendered *hors de combat* for the rest of the game.'

hors d'oeuvre: *(French)* literally, 'out of the main work'. It is the term given to a tasty preliminary dish at lunch or dinner. Example: 'We decided to skip the *hors d'oeuvre* because we were not very hungry.'

in extenso: *(Latin)* 'in full' or 'in detail'. Example: 'Shaw's *Back to Methuselah* is very rarely presented *in extenso* as it lasts for over six hours.'

infra dignitatem: *(Latin)* below one's dignity. The phrase is mostly used in its colloquial form, abbreviated to *infra dig*. Example: 'After winning his cricket Blue at Oxford, the silly young fool considered it to be *infra dig* to turn out for the village team in the vacation.'

in loco parentis: *(Latin)* in the place of a parent. This is a legal term defining the status of a Principal in relation to his pupils. Example: 'The headmaster was acting *in loco parentis* while John's parents were abroad.'

jeu d'esprit: *(French)* a witticism. Example: ' "Madam, I can resist everything except temptation", declared Oscar Wilde. With an occasional *jeu d'esprit* like this, Wilde was assured of invitations to the best dinner tables in London.'

laissez faire: *(French)* let matters be. This term is frequently used to describe government policy, when events are permitted to take their course. Example: 'The government adopted a *laissez faire* policy towards the colour problem, until events forced their hand in the 1960s.'

locum tenens: (*Latin*) someone holding another's place; a substitute or deputy. The term is usually abbreviated to '*locum*'. Example: 'My doctor is away on holiday next month, but he has managed to get a *locum* to run the surgery in his absence.'

mutatis mutandis: (*Latin*) the necessary changes being made. The term is often used in discussion or argument in making a comparison or in drawing an analogy which is not exact in every respect. Example: 'The complicated colour problem that first bedevilled American home politics some fifty years ago, has now – *mutatis mutandis* – enmeshed politics in Great Britain.'

née: (*French*) born. The term is frequently used in public notices of marriages and deaths, where it indicates the woman's maiden name. Example: 'Mrs Jane Fowler (*née* Talbot) died peacefully at her home last week.'

non sequitur: (*Latin*) it does not follow. Example: 'Recently I read in the newspapers, "Radio transmissions clearly influence climatic conditions, for within days of the changes in wavelengths by the BBC in November 1978, the temperature dropped about twenty degrees, and winter set in almost overnight." This piece of reasoning is clearly a *non sequitur*.' (It is also an example of the logical fallacy which is listed below – *post hoc* is not *propter hoc*.)

obiit: (*Latin*) 'he or she died'. This term appears on tombstones and in biographies, indicating the date and year of death. Example: 'Samuel Peckover, 86 years of age, *obiit* 3 January 1896.'

obiter dictum: (*Latin*) a passing or incidental comment. This is primarily a legal term referring to remarks made by a judge aside from the legal point at issue; hence it means any 'off the record' comment. Plural: *obiter dicta*. Example: ' "Tax evasion has now become a national pastime", declared Justice Strange in an *obiter dictum* that was widely reported.'

outré: (*French*) extravagant, in bad taste, eccentric. Example: 'His rather *outré* dress and behaviour upset the villagers.'

persona grata: (*Latin*) a person in favour, a welcome guest. Example: 'There are certain tennis players who are no longer *persona grata* at Wimbledon.'

pièce de resistance: (*French*) the principal course or item. Example: 'The *pièce de resistance* of the dinner party was roast turkey with all the trimmings.'

post hoc (is not) propter hoc: (*Latin*) 'after this' is not the same as 'because of this'. The terms refer to a logical fallacy similar to a *non sequitur* mentioned earlier. Example: 'Inflation rose after the Tories were elected, but the blame was not wholly theirs; *post hoc* is not *propter hoc*.'

post mortem: (*Latin*) after death. Usually applied to a medical examination of a corpse to determine the cause of death. Example: 'The court heard the result of the *post mortem*.'

pro tempore: (*Latin*) for the time being, temporarily. The abbreviation *pro tem.* is frequently used in conversation. Example: 'If you will take on the post of Secretary *pro tem.*, it will keep the society going until a permanent appointment is made.'

qui vive: (*French*) on the alert. Example: 'You must be on the *qui vive* for tomorrow's important examination.'

raison d'être: (*French*) a reason for existence; an explanation. Example: 'Nowadays the *raison d'être* of politics seems to be nothing more than a lust for power.'

sauve qui peut: (*French*) let him save himself if he can. Example: 'The situation has now deteriorated so much that it is a case of *sauve qui peut*.'

savoir faire: (*French*) ability, know-how, skill, tact. Example: 'He was no novice in the ways of society; everyone was impressed with his *savoir faire*.'

sine die: (*Latin*) without an appointed day, indefinitely. This is a legal term. Example: 'The case was adjourned *sine die*.'

soi-disant: (*French*) 'self-styled'. Example: 'This *soi-disant* poet enjoyed no one's approval but his own.'

status quo: (*Latin*) literally, 'the state in which'; hence, 'as things are or were'. This was originally a legal term. Example: 'The entire committee resigned, but after some deliberation the *status quo* was restored.' (This means that the committee withdrew its resignation.)

tour de force: (*French*) a feat of strength or a performance of distinction. Example: 'The exercise on the high bar was the champion's *tour de force*; it was brilliant.'

Zeitgeist: (*German*) the spirit of the age. Example: 'At any one time writers and artists appear to reflect a *Zeitgeist* – a mood or philosophy that influences all of them.'

Exercises

The following exercises help to familiarise the student with a wide range of words and their meanings, particularly those that tend to present difficulties. The questions draw attention to similarities and differences, and compel the reader to concentrate on precise shades of meaning.

1. Write down the negative forms of the following words. Example: agreement – disagreement

   (a) regular, (b) satisfied, (c) provident, (d) enchanted, (e) enviable, (f) appear, (g) illusion, (h) realistic

2. Give one word for each of the following:
   (a) a person who studies the stars
   (b) a person who studies insects
   (c) a person who studies flowers and plants
   (d) a person who studies rocks
   (e) a person who studies the working of the mind
   (f) a person who studies handwriting
   (g) a person who stuffs the skins of animals

3. Write down five words (all beginning with the prefix 'hand') which have the following meanings: Example: A linen or cotton square carried in the pocket: *handkerchief*.
   (a) good-looking
   (b) a disadvantage or impediment
   (c) the making of objects like tables, book-ends or toys
   (d) a short treatise or manual
   (e) an implement to secure the arms of prisoners

4. Write down five words (all beginning with 'per') which have the following meanings:
   (a) holes in a piece of paper to facilitate tearing
   (b) a sweet-smelling scent
   (c) a plant that lives all through the year
   (d) betrayal or breach of faith
   (e) to drip a liquid through a filter

5. Write down the two words that do not belong to each series, and state in a few words the topic or subject to which, in each case, the series of four words refer.
   (a) ballad, jade, elegy, sonnet, ode, solo
   (b) brandy, grain, grog, ginger, rum, beer
   (c) fume, parsley, fennel, terrapin, thyme, sage
   (d) keel, rudder, pier, mast, dock, gunwale

(*e*) drawl, chisel, dope, plane, wrench, drill
(*f*) axle, duffel, gear, altimeter, brake, sump
(*g*) depository, church, synagogue, tabernacle, temple, chancery
(*h*) cassette, bassoon, tuba, radio, piccolo, flute

6. Write short sentences or phrases showing clearly the meaning and correct use of the following words, using them in the form given. Example:

    abrasive Sandpaper is abrasive and is used for smoothing down wooden surfaces (*or, figuratively*: He had an abrasive personality: he always rubbed people up the wrong way).

(*a*) sleek, slick, smooth, glossy
(*b*) glow, sparkle, glint, dazzle
(*c*) callous, insensitive, tough, obtuse
(*d*) rash, improvident, reckless, slapdash

7. From these words choose the correct ones to fill the gaps in the sentences that follow:

    prevaricate   procrastinate   proximate   proliferate
    prognosticate   prostrate   propagate

(*a*) A warm greenhouse will help to ...... seeds.
(*b*) You should not ......: do it now.
(*c*) He fell ...... with exhaustion.
(*d*) Please tell the whole truth; don't ......
(*e*) Once you start forming splinter groups, they are sure to ......

8. Give the antonyms of the following words:

(*a*) reliable, (*b*) reputable, (*c*) relevant, (*d*) legible, (*e*) respectful, (*f*) morality, (*g*) tasteful, (*h*) trust

9. Give one word for each of the following:

(*a*) a book of instructions for a car
(*b*) an illustrated travel booklet
(*c*) a book in which to keep photographs
(*d*) a T.V. story spread over a number of weeks
(*e*) a short pamphlet with a religious message

10. Write short sentences showing clearly the meaning of the following pairs of words. Example:

    desert: The desert was a waterless, barren waste-land.
    dessert: For dessert he was offered peaches or nectarines.

(*a*) historic and histrionic
(*b*) homily and homely
(*c*) descant and descent
(*d*) succession and secession

11. Explain briefly the difference in meaning and use of the four words in each of the following groups:

   (a) gadget, machine, contraption, apparatus
   (b) crusade, mission, expedition, invasion
   (c) story, history, memoir, legend
   (d) atlas, map, plan, chart
   (e) 'spiv', crook, gangster, swindler

12. Re-arrange each group of four words in order of strength or emphasis, beginning with the strongest:

   (a) order, suggestion, ultimatum, recommendation
   (b) angry, annoyed, bitter, furious
   (c) adore, like, admire, regard
   (d) shout, call, bellow, speak
   (e) weep, whimper, sob, cry
   (f) disturbing, outrageous, offensive, unsettling

13. Write two short phrases or sentences using the following words (i) as a noun and (ii) as a verb. Example:

   cement I have bought a bag of cement. (noun)
   The marriage will cement a friendship between our families. (verb)

(a) beat	(f) discharge	(k) address	(p) gorge
(b) break	(g) flag	(l) vault	(q) loaf
(c) club	(h) mould	(m) match	(r) peer
(d) counter	(i) nurse	(n) last	(s) screen
(e) court	(j) minister	(o) hatch	(t) prune

14. In a phrase or sentence use each of the following words as (a) a noun, (b) an adjective, and (c) a verb:

   fire   light   cross   express

15. Write phrases or sentences to illustrate the use of each of the following words, in the exact form given, as any two parts of speech. Name the part of speech in each of your examples and underline the syllable that carries the stress or accent. Example:

   perfect It was a perfect performance. (adjective)
   He will perfect the invention very soon. (verb)

(a) compact	(d) defile	(g) object	(j) refuse
(b) second	(e) contrast	(h) transfer	(k) absent
(c) minute	(f) present	(i) entrance	(l) subject

16. Write down the four pairs of synonyms from the following:

   brave   repudiate   talkative   fast
   reject   speedy   courageous   loquacious

17. Write down an antonym for each of the following:

(a) courageous, (b) loquacious, (c) lively, (d) exonerate, (e) scarcity, (f) detract, (g) fiendish, (h) malefactor

18. Write short phrases or sentences using homophones of the following words. Example:

cede   I shall sow my lettuce *seed* in March.

(a) soul, (b) heart, (c) pear, (d) right, (e) beach, (f) quire, (g) fowl, (h) rough, (i) flare, (j) plum

19. Write short phrases or sentences using the following words (a) literally and (b) metaphorically. You may alter the words for plurals and tenses. Example:

hammer   (a) He borrowed my hammer for his building operation.
                (b) We must hammer home this message.

(a) plough, (b) eclipse, (c) blaze, (d) sift, (e) jockey, (f) handle, (g) storm, (h) patch, (i) pillar, (j) pinch

20. Each of the following sets of words contains two synonyms. Write these down.

(a) rich, relevant, argument, affluent
(b) stupid, obstinate, oblique, stubborn
(c) compatible, accessible, feasible, practicable
(d) banter, insolvent, unsuitable, bankrupt
(e) pauper, tramp, poverty, vagabond
(f) shun, suit, avoid, avid
(g) tamper, tempt, allure, allot
(h) humility, adoration, ornamentation, homage
(i) scowl, chaff, chafe, frown
(j) loneliness, anxiety, solicitude, solitude

21. Choose, from the words in brackets, the correct word to fill the gap in each of the given sentences:

(a) I was a . . . . . . to the accident.
    (sightseer, viewer, spectator, witness)
(b) The vandals had no respect or decency; they . . . . . . the graveyard.
    (destroyed, demolished, desecrated, deteriorated)
(c) The bus was . . . . . . at the terminus.
    (stabilised, stagnating, stationary, statutory)
(d) In his misery he made a . . . . . . of despair.
    (movement, gesture, greeting, guess)

(e) We must strive to . . . . . . the conditions under which the poor are living.
(affect, mention, ameliorate, anticipate)

(f) He was a man of very . . . . . . views; always open-minded and progressive.
(literary, lucky, libellous, liberal)

(g) You must . . . . . . on the task in hand and forget the rest.
(consider, condescend, concentrate, concentric)

(h) The loiterer was behaving in a . . . . . . manner.
(dangerous, solicitous, mendacious, suspicious)

(i) We must take a . . . . . . view of his failings: only in this way can we help him.
(cheerful, changeable, charitable, challenging)

(j) He was extremely . . . . . .; he would believe anything you told him.
(affable, culpable, laughable, gullible)

22. Explain briefly the difference in meaning between the following pairs of words, and write short phrases or sentences illustrating their correct use in each case.

(a) disinterested, uninterested   (f) faction, fiction
(b) perquisite, requisite   (g) tactful, tactile
(c) discrete, discreet   (h) emulate, immolate
(d) abeyance, obeisance   (i) economy, ecology
(e) elusive, allusive   (j) dividend, divination

23. Use the following foreign phrases in sentences:

(a) *ad infinitum*   (d) *double entendre*   (g) *pro tem.*
(b) *carte blanche*   (e) *ex officio*   (h) *sine die*
(c) *curriculum vitae*   (f) *non sequitur*

24. Re-write the following sentences using an English phrase in place of the foreign one, and without radically changing the meaning:

(a) I'm afraid you are not *persona grata* with the committee.
(b) Jack plays pop records *ad nauseam*.
(c) *A propos* my earlier suggestion, I now think we should drop it.
(d) Strictly *entre nous* I must confess that these tickets are forged.
(e) She decided it was *infra dig.* for her to wait any longer.
(f) The situation was restored to the *status quo.*

Part 6

Figures of speech and common sayings

Figures of speech

Figures of speech are modes of expression that help to give colour, emphasis or vividness to the ideas being expressed. They have been employed by writers in all languages from earliest times. Nowadays, some of the names of the figures of speech are of academic interest only, but the figures themselves are still very much an intrinsic part of the language.

Simile

A simile is a figure of speech based on comparison, usually introduced by 'like' or 'as'. We all use similes in our everyday speech. Our first examples are of very common, everyday similes; though hackneyed, they nevertheless add colour to our speech:

as clean as a whistle
as dry as a bone
as good as gold
as poor as a churchmouse
as quick as lightning

as dead as a doornail
as dull as ditchwater
as heavy as lead
as proud as a peacock
as right as rain

In serious writing, however, you should always try to think up original comparisons. Here are a few examples of similes found in modern writing; they are often made memorable by their subtle observation, wit and humour:

Life is rather like a tin of sardines – we're all looking for the key.
Penelope has a penetrating laugh – rather like a train going into a tunnel.
Joe is a colourless personality; he goes about his business with as little uproar as a jelly-fish.
The new curate was terribly high-church; he trailed an aroma of piety like a whiff of after-shave.

Marriage is sometimes like a gift-wrapped time bomb.
In the paddock the jockeys were thrown into their saddles like confetti.

English poetry, of course, is studded with similes:

Look like the innocent flower,
But be the serpent under it. (Shakespeare)

The Assyrian came down like a wolf on the fold. (Byron)

Then felt I like some watcher of the skies
When a new planet swims into his ken. (Keats)

Metaphor

Metaphors are the most widely used of all figures of speech; they are used scores of times a day in everyone's conversation. Like the simile, a metaphor is based on comparison, but here it is closer still – a virtual identification of the items compared. For example, in the sentence 'The water was boiling', the word 'boiling' is used in a literal sense; but we can use the same word and idea very vividly in a figurative sense – that is, as a metaphor:

He was boiling with anger and took a long time to simmer down.

Here are some further simple examples:

Don't fish in troubled waters.
Between us we shall hammer out a solution.
The whole affair was wrapped in secrecy.
Stories of Dracula make the flesh creep.
Noah was the first successful business tycoon; he floated a limited company while the rest of the world was in liquidation. (The metaphors here also conceal puns.)

Again, we find English prose and poetry throughout the centuries enlivened and enriched by the use of metaphor:

juicy pears that cheat the teeth. (Edmund Blunden)

O for a beaker full of the warm South . . .
With beaded bubbles winking at the brim. (Keats)

                    We are such stuff
As dreams are made on, and our little life
Is rounded with a sleep. (Shakespeare)

Gather ye rosebuds while ye may,
Old Time is still a-flying,
And this same flower that smiles today,
Tomorrow will be dying. (Herrick)

The winter evening settles down
With smells of steaks in passageways.
Six o'clock.
The burnt-out ends of smoky days. (T. S. Eliot)

Along the wind-swept platform, pinched and white,
The travellers stand in pools of wintry light,
Offering themselves to morn's long, slanting arrows.
(Siegfried Sassoon)

I cannot praise a fugitive and cloistered virtue, unexercised and
unbreathed, that never sallies out and sees her adversary . . . (Milton)

Antithesis

This is a figure of speech based on contrasts;

Marry in haste; repent at leisure.
A bright eye indicates some curiosity; a black eye, too much.
Genius does what it must; talent, what it can.
Lessons are not given; they are taken.

Oxymoron

Literally, this means 'sharp-dull' and it involves a more extreme contrast
than antithesis. Indeed, oxymoron often involves an apparent
contradiction:

an honest rogue   a painful pleasure   a quiet noise

Many poets employ oxymoron as these quotations from Shakespeare
and Tennyson illustrate:

with mirth in funeral and with dirge in marriage.   (Shakespeare)

His honour rooted in dishonour stood,
And faith unfaithful kept him falsely true.   (Tennyson)

Paradox

This involves a seemingly contradictory statement. It is very similar to
oxymoron but often hides a novel truth:

Honesty is a luxury for the tycoon, but a necessity for the cloakroom
attendant.
If a thing is worth doing, it's worth doing badly.
The child is father of the man.

Epigram

An epigram is a short, witty saying, often with an edge of satire.
Epigrams are easy to remember and, for this reason, are often used to
emphasise a point.

As far as motoring is concerned, it is the overtaker who keeps the undertaker busy.
Better late than 'the late'.
I can resist everything but temptation.
An atheist is a man with no invisible means of support.
Be patient; in time even an egg will walk.

Euphemism

This involves the use of a mild and gentle expression to conceal a harsh reality:

he passed away   (he died)
a terminological inexactitude   (a blatant lie)
battlefield wastage   (the dead and maimed in battle)
clothes for the fuller figure   (clothes for fat people).

Hyperbole

This figure of speech involves gross exaggeration. It is often used by humorous writers:

He was a tough guy; he shaved with a blow-torch.
I spent a year in that town – on Sunday.
I'm so hungry I could eat a horse.

Litotes

This involves the use of understatement:

Shakespeare's *Othello* is quite a good tragedy.
There was a spot of bother at the football match when the referee awarded a penalty.
He lives in comfortable circumstances.

Onomatopoeia

The use of words whose sound suggests their meaning: *boom, crack, slap, splash.* Comics frequently employ onomatopoeic items such as *wham!, bam!, boi-ing!, pow!* and *zip!*

But onomatopoeia can be subtly used in poetry, as in 'the tintinnabulation of the bells' where the sounds of the words echo their sense.

Alliteration

This is not a figure of speech but is so frequently found in poetry that it deserves a comment. It involves the repetition of the same consonant:

He was bewitched, bothered and bewildered.
Round and round the rugged rocks the ragged rascal ran.

O, she doth teach the torches to burn bright. (Shakespeare)
Landscape plotted and pieced – fold, fallow and plough.
(Gerard Manley Hopkins)

Among British poets Tennyson is probably best known for effectively combining alliteration with onomatopoeia:

Dry clashed his harness in the icy caves
And barren chasms, and all to left and right
The bare black cliff clanged round him as he based
His feet on juts of slippery crag that rang
Sharp smitten with the dint of armed heels . . . (from *Morte D'Arthur*)

Sweeter thy voice, but every sound is sweet;
Myriads of rivulets hurrying through the lawn,
The moan of doves in immemorial elms
And murmuring of innumerable bees . . . (from *The Princess*)

Exercises

1. Name the figures of speech – sometimes more than one – in each of the following:
   (a) The ploughman homewards plods his weary way.
   (b) The song had a bitter-sweet melancholy about it.
   (c) Man proposes; God disposes.
   (d) I heard the crack of the rifle, followed by the zing of the ricochet.
   (e) Life today is something of a rat-race.
   (f) The sportscar zoomed into the garage.
   (g) He clowned his way through life.
   (h) The fellow grinned at me like a half-wit.
   (i) The policeman shepherded the children across the busy road.
   (j) Inflation is like sin; every government denounces it and every government practises it.

2. Turn to the passage from R. L. Stevenson on pp. 112–13 entitled *My Shore Adventure* and answer the following questions:
   (a) Write down and name the words or phrases that are figures of speech in the last two sentences in the first paragraph, beginning 'The hills ran up clear' and ending 'to put a statue on'.
   (b) Indicate and name the figures of speech employed in the second sentence of the second paragraph, beginning 'The booms were tearing at the blocks' and ending 'like a manufactory'.
   (c) Indicate and name the figure of speech employed in the last twenty-four words of the third paragraph.
   (d) Indicate and name the figures of speech to be found in the last eight lines of the final paragraph of the passage.

Proverbial and common sayings

The English language is rich in proverbial and common sayings, some dating back many centuries. Though, in a sense, these expressions are well-worn clichés, they can nevertheless add point or humour to a situation in which they are used. There are many thousands of these expressions and we can only give a typical selection of some of the best known. Students who are studying English as a foreign language will find that a knowledge of these proverbs and sayings will be helpful to them in their understanding and command of idiomatic English.

The proverbs and sayings are listed below without explanation, as the majority of them, in their picturesque way, are immediately self-evident. The difficulties arise when you try to explain their meaning clearly to somebody. No doubt it is because of this that in many English Language examinations candidates are asked to explain some of these sayings, or to devise a context in which the proverb or saying could appropriately be used, as in the following examples:

(1) 'An iron hand in a velvet glove.'

This means that a person may give an outward appearance of gentleness and reasonable behaviour, but underneath there is a stern or even ruthless determination to get what he wants.

Illustration of its use:

A cunning dictator often plays up to the subservient masses by projecting an image of a kindly, considerate father of his people; but it is well for the populace to remember that there is an iron hand in the velvet glove.

(2) 'By hook or by crook.'

This means by one way or another; if one approach fails, you will try another.

Illustration of its use:

I will never forgive him for what he has done to me, and by hook or by crook I will get my own back on him.

(3) 'Too many cooks spoil the broth.'

This means that you can confuse and muddle a task if you have too many people working at it.

Illustration of its use:

Look here, Peter and John, it doesn't need all of you to do that; just get out of the way and let David do the job on his own – too many cooks spoil the broth, you know.

LIST OF COMMON SAYINGS

A bull in a china shop
A nine-days' wonder
A stitch in time saves nine
A storm in a tea-cup
A watched pot never boils
A willing horse
All his geese are swans
All that glitters is not gold
All tarred with the same brush
All's well that ends well
An iron hand in a velvet glove
An old head on young shoulders
Any port in a storm

Barking up the wrong tree
Beating about the bush
Beauty is only skin deep
Beggars can't be choosers
Better safe than sorry
Between the devil and the deep blue sea
Between you, me and the gatepost
Birds of a feather flock together
Blood is thicker than water
Bringing coals to Newcastle
By hook or by crook

Cast ne'er a clout till May is out
Charity begins at home
Cut your coat according to your cloth

Dead men tell no tales
Discretion is the better part of valour
Do as you would be done by
Do not keep a dog and bark yourself
Do not meet troubles half-way
Do not put all your eggs in one basket
Dog does not eat dog

Easy come, easy go
Empty vessels make most sound
Enough is as good as a feast
Even a worm will turn
Every cloud has a silver lining
Every dog has its day

Familiarity breeds contempt

Forewarned is forearmed
From pillar to post

Give a dog a bad name and hang him
Give him an inch, he'll take a mile
Give the devil his due

Half a loaf is better than no bread
Have an eye to the main chance
He cannot say boo to a goose
He has not a penny to bless himself with
He makes a rod for his own back
He who pays the piper may call the tune
His bark is worse than his bite
Honesty is the best policy

I have other fish to fry
If you can't stand the heat, stay out of the kitchen
It is easy to be wise after the event
It is no use crying over spilt milk
It never rains but it pours
It's a long lane that has no turning

Jack is as good as his master
Jack of all trades and master of none

Least said, soonest mended
Let bygones be bygones
Let sleeping dogs lie
Let the cobbler stick to his last
Like a dying duck in a thunderstorm
Like a fish out of water
Like a house on fire
Like a red rag to a bull
Like water off a duck's back
Look before you leap

Make hay while the sun shines
More haste, less speed

Necessity is the mother of invention
No news is good news
Nothing succeeds like success
Nothing ventured, nothing gained

Once bitten, twice shy
One good turn deserves another
One man's meat is another man's poison

One swallow does not make a summer
Out of the frying pan, into the fire

Penny wise, pound foolish
People who live in glass houses should not throw stones
Put your shoulder to the wheel

Rome was not built in a day

Set a thief to catch a thief
Six of one and half a dozen of the other
Slow but sure
Spare the rod and spoil the child
Still waters run deep
Strike while the iron is hot

The fat is in the fire
The pot calls the kettle black
The proof of the pudding is in the eating
The road to hell is paved with good intentions
The sting in the tail
The straw that breaks the camel's back
The thin end of the wedge
The world is his oyster
There is no smoke without fire
There's many a slip 'twixt the cup and the lip
To be born with a silver spoon in one's mouth
To blow one's own trumpet
To build castles in Spain
To burn one's boats
To burn the candle at both ends
To buy a pig in a poke
To call a spade a spade
To count one's chickens before they are hatched
To cut off one's nose to spite one's face
To flog a dead horse
To have a bee in one's bonnet
To have a finger in the pie
To have a rod in pickle for someone
To have bats in the belfry
To have too many irons in the fire
To help a lame dog over a stile
To hit the nail on the head
To keep one's nose to the grindstone
To kill the goose that lays the golden eggs
To kill two birds with one stone

To know on which side one's bread is buttered
To let the cat out of the bag
To lick into shape
To look as if butter wouldn't melt in one's mouth
To look for a needle in a haystack
To make a mountain out of a molehill
To pour oil on troubled waters
To put the cart before the horse
To rob Peter to pay Paul
To run with the hare and hunt with the hounds
To see which way the cat jumps
To set the Thames on fire
To shut the stable door after the horse has gone
To sow one's wild oats
To split hairs
To spoil the ship for a ha'porth of tar
To take one down a peg or two
To take the bull by the horns
To take the rough with the smooth
Two wrongs do not make a right

Waste not, want not
What is sauce for the goose is sauce for the gander
When in Rome, do as the Romans do
Where there's a will, there's a way

You cannot get blood out of a stone
You cannot have your cake and eat it
You cannot make a silk purse out of a sow's ear
You cannot make an omelet without breaking eggs
You cannot see the wood for the trees
You cannot teach an old dog new tricks
You can take a horse to water but you cannot make him drink
You could have knocked me down with a feather

Exercises

1. Re-write the following sentences substituting your own words for the
   proverbial expressions printed in italic – as in this example:

   Don't believe all that John tells you; you must allow for the fact
   that *all his geese are swans.*

   > *Answer:*   Don't believe all that John tells you; remember that he
   > tends to exaggerate and see things as being better than
   > they are.

(a) I'm sure Peter will do the job for you; he is always a *willing horse*.

(b) Now that you are out of work you will have to *cut your coat according to your cloth*.

(c) When you invest your savings, be sure not to *put all yours eggs in one basket*.

(d) You have had a run of bad luck, but *every cloud has a silver lining*.

(e) He always means well and swears he will help you, but *the road to hell is paved with good intentions*.

(f) It's no good bearing a grudge against your former friend; you should *let bygones be bygones*.

(g) Marriage is a very serious commitment: I advise you to *look before you leap*.

(h) He was told to keep the matter secret, but the silly boy *let the cat out of the bag*.

(i) I'm afraid old John is very settled in his ways: *you cannot teach an old dog new tricks*.

2. Can you find a proverbial saying to suit the situation suggested in the following sentences?

(a) I was never so surprised in my life.

(b) Before making up your mind you had better see how the majority vote.

(c) After the burglary he fitted all sorts of locks and alarm systems, but it was then too late.

(d) It is no good bewailing your bad luck, for we all have moments of success and moments of failure; you must learn to live with both.

(e) The silly fellow is taking on too much; he plays football three times a week, goes swimming twice, plays billiards, sings in the local choir and is trying to work for a degree.

(f) She looks very quiet and demure, as if she could never be angry.

(g) Some readers enjoy thrillers; others just cannot stand them – it shows how tastes can differ.

(h) He sounds a very fierce person, but actually he is reasonable and gentle.

Part 7

Some paragons of English prose

IT IS APPROPRIATE NOW to look at a few examples of good English prose. In the course of our studies so far we have examined the nature of sentences and their various structures; we have considered problems of syntax, that is, the application of the rules of grammar to sentence construction, and we have observed the influence of vocabulary and punctuation on the writing of English prose. The next step is to see how all these complex elements can be reconciled and balanced by an author in an actual piece of writing. To this end we shall study a few extracts from the works of eminent writers over a span of four centuries.

First it is essential to realise that there are many kinds of good writing; excellence depends largely on the degree of suitability of the writer's style for the audience he has in mind. His readers may be ordinary people without any pretensions to literary scholarship, or they may be intellectuals, academics or specialists in various fields. For this reason our criteria of judgement must be flexible and accommodating, and must take the writer's aims and intentions into account.

Daniel Defoe

Daniel Defoe (1661–1731) won fame in his day as a political writer, but it is as the author of *A Journal of the Plague Year* (1722) and the *Adventures of Robinson Crusoe* (1719) that he has been valued and remembered as one of the greatest writers of clear English prose. He writes for the ordinary reader and his prose style is accordingly simple, vivid and direct – a model of clarity that is worthy of close study today. The extract quoted is from the journal Robinson Crusoe kept while struggling to survive on the remote island on which he had been shipwrecked. A few unusual words and turns of phrase reflect the language that was in use over three hundred years ago. Even so, the writing presents little or no difficulty today.

CRUSOE'S JOURNAL

September 30, 1659. I, poor miserable Robinson Crusoe, being shipwrecked during a dreadful storm, in the offing, came on shore on this dismal unfortunate island, which I call the *Island of Despair*; all the rest of the ship's company being drowned, and myself almost dead.

October 1. In the morning I saw, to my great surprise, the ship had floated with the high tide, and was driven on shore again much nearer the island. I hoped, if the wind abated, I might get on board, and get some food and necessaries out of her for my relief. I spent great part of this day in perplexing myself on these things; but, at length, seeing the ship almost dry, I went upon the sand as near as I could, and then swam on board. This day also it continued raining, though with no wind at all.

From the *1st* of *October* to the *24th*. All these days entirely spent in many several voyages to get all I could out of the ship; which I brought on shore, every tide of flood, upon rafts. Much rain also in these days, though with some intervals of fair weather: but it seems this was the rainy season.

Oct. 25. It rained all night and all day, with some gusts of wind; during which time the ship broke in pieces (the wind blowing a little harder than before) and was no more to be seen, except the wreck of her, and that only at low water. I spent this day in covering and securing the goods which I had saved, that the rain might not spoil them.

From the *26th* to the *30th*, I worked very hard in carrying my goods to my habitation, though some part of the time it rained exceedingly hard.

The *31st*, in the morning, I went out into the island with my gun, to see for some food, and discover the country; when I killed a she-goat, and her kid followed me home, which I afterwards killed also, because it would not feed.

November 1. I set up my tent under a rock, and lay there for the first night; making it as large as I could, with stakes driven in to swing my hammock upon.

Nov 4. This morning I began to order my times of work, of going out with my gun, time to sleep, and time of diversion; viz., every morning I walked out with my gun for two or three hours, if it did not rain; then employed myself to work till about eleven o'clock; then eat what I had to live on; and from twelve to two I lay down to sleep, the weather being excessively hot; and then, in the evening, to work again. The working part of the day and the next was wholly employed in making my table, for I was as yet but a very sorry workman: though time and necessity made me a complete natural mechanic soon after, as I believe they would any one else.

Nov. 13. This day it rained; which refreshed me exceedingly, and cooled the earth: but it was accompanied with terrible thunder and lightning, which frightened me dreadfully, for fear of my powder. As soon as it was over I resolved to separate my stock of powder into as many little parcels as possible, that it might not be in danger.

Nov. 17. This day I began to dig behind my tent, into the rock, to make room for my further convenience. *Note.* Three things I wanted exceedingly for this work, viz., a pickaxe, a shovel, and a wheelbarrow, or basket: so I desisted from my work, and began to consider how to supply these wants, and make me some tools. As for pickaxe, I made use of the iron crows, which were proper enough, though heavy: but the next thing was a shovel or spade; this was so absolutely necessary, that, indeed, I could do nothing effectually without it; but what kind of one to make I knew not.

Nov. 18. The next day, in searching the woods, I found a tree of that wood, or like it, which, in the Brazils, they call the iron tree, from its exceeding hardness: of this, with great labour, and almost spoiling my axe, I cut a piece; and brought it home, too, with difficulty enough, for it was exceeding heavy. The excessive hardness of the wood, and my having no other way, made me a long while upon this machine: for I worked it effectually by little and little, into the form of a shovel or spade; the handle exactly shaped like ours in England, only that the broad part having no iron shod upon it at the bottom, it would not last me so long; however, it served well enough for the uses which I had occasion to put it to; but never was a shovel, I believe, made after that fashion, or so long in making.

The above extract is a classic example of simple, effective prose. You will have noticed that Defoe's punctuation is decidedly old-fashioned; today we employ fewer stops. He also uses a limited vocabulary, repeating words like 'exceeding' and 'exceedingly', 'effectual' and 'effectually' and 'excessive'. Even so, his prose is still attractive and evocative.

Jonathan Swift

Jonathan Swift (1667–1745) won early fame as a controversial writer in the fields of religion and politics, and soon grew in reputation for his mastery of satire and irony. He is best remembered for the biting satire of *Gulliver's Travels* (1726), though the work has survived mainly as a children's book. In *Gulliver's Travels* he pitilessly exposes the meanness, vanity and unscrupulousness of people in authority, from kings to petty officials. Swift's greatness shows in the richness of his allegorical invention, in his humour and irony, and in the lucidity, ease and precision of his prose style. Nowhere are these qualities better seen than in *Gulliver's Travels*, from which the following short extract has been taken.

THE COURT OF LILLIPUT

The emperor had a mind one day to entertain me with several of the country shows, wherein they exceed all nations I have known, both for dexterity and magnificence. I was diverted by none so much as that of the rope-dancers, performed with a slender white thread extended about two feet and twelve inches from the ground. Upon which I shall desire liberty, with the reader's patience, to enlarge a little.

This diversion is only practised by those persons who are candidates for great employments and high favour at court. They are trained in this art from their youth, and are not always of noble birth or liberal education. When a great office is vacant, either by death or disgrace (which often happens), five or six of those candidates petition the emperor to entertain his majesty and the court with a dance on the rope; and whoever jumps the highest, without falling, succeeds in the office. Very often the chief ministers themselves are commanded to shew their skill, and to convince the emperor that they have not lost their faculty. Flimnap, the treasurer, is allowed to cut a caper on the straight rope at least an inch higher than any other lord in the whole empire. I have seen him do the summerset several times together upon a trencher fixed on a rope which is no thicker than a common pack-thread in England. My friend Reldresal, principal secretary for private affairs is, in my opinion, if I am not partial, the second after the treasurer; the rest of the great officers are much upon a par.

These diversions are often attended with fatal accidents, whereof great numbers are on record. I myself have seen two or three candidates break a limb. But the danger is much greater when the ministers themselves are commanded to show their dexterity; for by contending to excel themselves and their fellows, they strain so far that there is hardly one of them who has not received a fall, and some of them two or three. I was assured that, a year or two before my arrival, Flimnap would infallibly have broke his neck if one of the king's cushions that accidentally lay on the ground had not weakened the force of his fall.

There is likewise another diversion, which is only shown before the emperor and empress and first minister, upon particular occasions. The emperor lays on the table three fine silken threads, of six inches long; one is blue, the other red, and the third green. These threads are proposed as prizes for those persons the emperor has a mind to distinguish by a peculiar mark of his favour. The ceremony is performed in his majesty's great chamber of state, where the candidates are to undergo a trial of dexterity, very different from the former, and such as I have not observed the least resemblance of in any other country of the new or old world. The emperor holds a stick in his hands, both ends parallel to the horizon, while the candidates, advancing one by one, sometimes leap over the stick, sometimes creep under it, backward and forward, several times, according as the stick is advanced or depressed. Sometimes the emperor holds one end of the stick, and his first minister the other; sometimes the minister has it entirely to himself. Whoever performs his part with most agility, and holds out the longest in leaping and creeping, is rewarded with the blue-coloured silk; the red is given to the next, and the green to the third, which they all wear girt twice round about the middle, and you see few great persons about this court who are not adorned with one of these girdles.

In the above extract we have another example of lucid, simple prose, artfully contrived to read as a dispassionate, matter-of-fact account of Gulliver's strange experiences. Once again we observe the old-fashioned mode of punctuation, but the sense is crystal clear, the vocabulary being straightforward and in no way archaic. The satirical element in the passage is like a time-bomb; upon reflection we are struck by its full meaning, which is as relevant today as it was nearly three hundred years ago.

Joseph Addison

Joseph Addison (1672–1719) was a contemporary of both Defoe and Swift, but in many ways he belongs to another world. He was a classicist, an academic and a humanist in outlook, and his style reflects the restrained elegance of classical values. His literary career began as a poet, but it was as an essayist and writer of well-turned prose that his reputation was established. He co-operated with Richard Steele in writing for the journals *The Tatler* (1709–11) and *The Spectator* (1711–12). Addison was a man of affairs and became Secretary of State in 1717, but by temperament and inclination he most enjoyed living the life of a middle-class man of letters. In *The Spectator* he ignored political and religious controversy, preferring to write eassays in a gentle didactic tone, commenting with charm and grace upon the social life of the day.

The following extract from issue No. 10 of *The Spectator* clearly reveals Addison's ideals and his civilised, urbane style.

ON *THE SPECTATOR*

It is with much satisfaction that I hear this great city inquiring day by day after these my papers, and receiving my morning lectures with a becoming seriousness and attention. My publisher tells me that there are already three thousand of them distributed every day: so that if I allow twenty readers to every paper, which I look upon as a modest computation, I may reckon about three score thousand disciples in London and Westminster, who I hope will take care to distinguish themselves from the thoughtless herd of their ignorant and inattentive brethren. Since I have raised to myself so great an audience, I shall spare no pains to make their instruction agreeable, and their diversion useful. For which reasons I shall endeavour to enliven morality with wit, and to temper wit with morality, that my readers may, if possible, both ways find their account in the speculation of the day. And to the end that their virtue and discretion may not be short, transient, intermitting starts of thought, I have resolved to refresh their memories from day to day, till I have recovered them out of that desperate state of vice and folly into which the age has fallen. The mind that lies fallow but a single day, sprouts up in follies that are only to be killed by a constant and assiduous culture. It was said of Socrates that he brought Philosophy down from heaven, to inhabit among men: and I shall be ambitious to have it said of me, that I have brought Philosophy out of closets and libraries, schools and colleges, to dwell in clubs and assemblies, at tea-tables and in coffee-houses.

I would therefore in a very particular manner recommend these my speculations to all well-regulated families that set apart an hour of every morning for tea and bread and butter; and would earnestly advise them for their good to order this paper to be punctually served up, and to be looked upon as a part of the tea equipage . . . I shall not be so vain as to think that where the *Spectator* appears the other public prints will vanish; but shall leave it to my readers' consideration whether is it not much better to be let into the knowledge of one's self than to hear what passes in Muscovy or Poland, and to amuse ourselves with such writings as tend to the wearing out of ignorance, passion and prejudice, than such as naturally conduce to inflame hatreds and make enmities irreconcilable.

But there are none to whom this paper will be more useful than to the female world. I have often thought there has not been sufficient pains taken in finding out proper employments and diversions for the fair ones. Their amusements seem contrived for them, rather as they are women than as they are reasonable creatures; and are more adapted to the sex than to the species. The toilet is their great scene of business, and the right adjusting of their hair the principal employment of their lives. The sorting of a suit of ribbons is reckoned a very good morning's work; and if they make an excursion to a mercer's or a toy-shop, so great a fatigue makes them unfit for anything else all the day after. Their more serious occupations are sewing and embroidery, and their greatest drudgery the preparation of jellies and sweet-meats. This, I say, is the state of ordinary women; though I know there are multitudes of those of a more elevated life and conversation, that move in an exalted sphere of knowledge and virtue, that join all the beauties of the mind to the ornaments of dress, and inspire a kind of awe and respect, as well as love, into their male beholders. I hope to increase the number of these by publishing this daily paper, which I shall always endeavour to make an innocent if not an improving entertainment, and by that means at least divert the minds of my female readers from greater trifles.

Robert Louis Stevenson

With R.L. Stevenson (1850–94) we have jumped 170 years from the age of Defoe, Swift and Addison, but the English language has not changed significantly; it is somewhat more sophisticated, as we shall see, but its simplicity and clarity are preserved in the writings of Stevenson, a writer who won a reputation as an essayist, literary critic, journalist and finally as a novelist.

The extracts chosen are from his *Travels with a Donkey in the Cevennes* (1879) and from *Treasure Island* (1883), one of the best adventure stories for boys ever written. Few writers have given such attention to problems of style. Stevenson chooses his words with scrupulous precision, and listens carefully to the rhythms, cadences and general harmony of his sentences. He shapes his prose style to the audience he has in mind: he can write as effectively for a critical academic audience as he can for more youthful readers. At all times his prose is beautifully tempered – an excellent model for everyone to study and enjoy.

TRAVELS WITH A DONKEY

The whole descent is like a dream to me, so rapidly was it accomplished. I had scarcely left the summit ere the valley had closed round my path, and the sun beat upon me, walking in a stagnant lowland atmosphere. The track became a road, and went up and down in easy undulations. I passed cabin after cabin, but all seemed deserted; and I saw not a human creature nor heard any sound except that of the stream. I was, however, in a different country from the day before. The stony skeleton of the world was here vigorously displayed to sun and air. The slopes were steep and changeful. Oak-trees clung along the hills, well grown, wealthy in leaf, and touched by the autumn with strong and luminous colours. Here and there another stream would fall in from the right or the left, down a gorge of snow-white and tumultuary boulders. The river in the bottom (for it was rapidly growing a river, collecting on all hands as it trotted on its way) here foamed a while in desperate rapids, and there lay in pools of the most enchanting sea-green shot with watery browns. As far as I have gone, I have never seen a river of so changeful and delicate a hue;

crystal was not more clear, the meadows were not by half so green; and at every pool I saw I felt a thrill of longing to be out of these hot, dusty, and material garments, and bathe my naked body in the mountain air and water.

MY SHORE ADVENTURE

The appearance of the island when I came on deck next morning was altogether changed. Although the breeze had now utterly failed, we had made a great deal of way during the night, and were now lying becalmed about half a mile to the south-east of the low eastern coast. Grey-coloured woods covered a large part of the surface. This even tint was indeed broken up by streaks of yellow sandbreak in the lower lands, and by many tall trees of the pine family, out-topping the others – some singly, some in clumps; but the general colouring was uniform and sad. The hills ran up clear above the vegetation in spires of naked rock. All were strangely shaped, and the Spy-glass, which was by three or four hundred feet the tallest on the island, was likewise the strangest in configuration, running up sheer from almost every side, and then suddenly cut off at the top like a pedestal to put a statue on.

The *Hispaniola* was rolling scuppers under in the ocean swell. The booms were tearing at the blocks, the rudder was banging to and fro, and the whole ship creaking, groaning, and jumping like a manufactory. I had to cling tight to the backstay, and the world turned giddily before my eyes; for though I was a good enough sailor when there was way on, this standing still and being rolled about like a bottle was a thing I never learned to stand without a qualm or so, above all in the morning, on an empty stomach.

Perhaps it was this – perhaps it was the look of the island with its grey, melancholy woods, and wild stone spires, and the surf that we could both see and hear foaming and thundering on the steep beach – at least, although the sun shone bright and hot, and the shore birds were fishing and crying all around us, and you would have thought anyone would have been glad to get to land after being so long at sea, my heart sank, as the saying is, into my boots; and from that first look onward, I hated the very thought of Treasure Island.

We had a dreary morning's work before us, for there was no sign of any wind, and the boats had to be got out and manned, and the ship warped three or four miles round the corner of the island, and up the narrow passage to the haven behind Skeleton Island. I volunteered for one of the boats, where I had, of course, no business. The heat was sweltering, and the men grumbled fiercely over their work. Anderson was in command of my boat, and instead of keeping the crew in order, he grumbled as loud as the worst.

'Well,' he said, with an oath, 'it's not for ever.'

I thought this was a very bad sign; for, up to that day, the men had gone briskly and willingly about their business; but the very sight of the island had relaxed the cords of discipline.

All the way in, Long John stood by the steersman and conned the ship. He knew the passage like the palm of his hand; and though the man in the chains got everywhere more water than was down in the chart, John never hesitated once.

'There's a strong scour with the ebb,' he said, 'and this here passage has been dug out, in a manner of speaking, with a spade.'

We brought up just where the anchor was in the chart, about a third of a mile from either shore, the mainland on one side, and Skeleton Island on the other. The bottom was clean sand. The plunge of our anchor sent up clouds of birds wheeling and crying over the woods; but in less than a minute they were down again, and all was once more silent.

The place was entirely land-locked, buried in woods, the trees coming right down to high-water mark, the shores mostly flat, and the hill-tops standing round at a distance in a sort of amphitheatre, one here, one there. Two little rivers, or, rather, two swamps, emptied out into this pond, as you might call it; and the foliage round that part of the shore had a kind of poisonous brightness. From the ship, we could see nothing of the house or stockade, for they were quite buried among trees; and if it had not been for the chart on the companion, we might have been the first that had ever anchored there since the island arose out of the seas. There was not a breath of air moving, nor a sound but that of the surf booming half a mile away along the beaches and against the rocks outside. A peculiar stagnant smell hung over the anchorage – a smell of sodden leaves and rotting tree trunks. I observed the doctor sniffing and sniffing, like someone tasting a bad egg.

'I don't know about treasure,' he said, 'but I'll stake my wig there's fever here.'

William Golding

William Golding (*b.*1911) is the author of a number of well-written novels and plays, among which his *Lord of the Flies* (1954) is perhaps the best known. It is a disturbing story of a party of young boys who are stranded on a remote Pacific island, following a plane crash. Without guidance and a society to hold them together, the boys gradually revert to a state of savagery and supersitition. The story is simply told, the characters sharply drawn and the terrain evocatively described in a style that is direct, vivid and clear.

Our extract is from the opening chapter in which we meet two of the survivors – the fair boy in his school sweater, grey shirt and socks, mature and confident for his age, and his fat companion, uncouth in speech and appearance, bespectacled and wearing a greasy old wind-cheater. From the start the characters are sharply differentiated and the strange atmosphere of the island established.

SURVIVORS

The boy with fair hair lowered himself down the last few feet of rock and began to pick his way towards the lagoon. Though he had taken off his school sweater and trailed it now from one hand, his grey shirt stuck to him and his hair was plastered to his forehead. All round him the long scar smashed into the jungle was a bath of heat. He was clambering heavily among the creepers and broken trunks when a bird, a vision of red and yellow, flashed upwards with a witch-like cry; and this cry was echoed by another.

'Hi!' it said, 'wait a minute!'

The undergrowth at the side of the scar was shaken and a multitude of raindrops fell pattering.

'Wait a minute,' the voice said, 'I got caught up.'

The fair boy stopped and jerked his stockings with an automatic gesture that made the jungle seem for a moment like the Home Counties.

The voice spoke again.

'I can't hardly move with all these creeper things.'

The owner of the voice came backing out of the undergrowth so that twigs scratched on a greasy wind-breaker. The naked crooks of his knees were plump, caught and scratched by thorns. He bent down, removed the thorns carefully, and turned round. He was shorter than the fair boy and very fat. He came forward, searching out safe lodgements for his feet, and then looked up through thick spectacles.

'Where's the man with the megaphone?'

The fair boy shook his head.

'This is an island. At least I think it's an island. That's a reef out in the sea. Perhaps there aren't any grown-ups anywhere . . . .'

Graham Greene

Graham Greene (*b*.1905) is a distinguished modern author. He has written over thirty novels, travel books, children's books, essays and short stories. His novels, though serious, have a wide popular appeal and more than a dozen have been made into films.

The brief extract chosen is from Chapter 2 of *The Human Factor* (1978), a spy story that is tense, moving, amusing and, above all, beautifully written. His central character is Maurice Castle, an unsuspected secret agent who eventually defects to Russia, losing his family and friends in the process. We meet him here as a seemingly innocent commuter, making his regular, uneventful way home from the Foreign Office to join his wife, Sarah, and his stepson, Sam.

This account of Castle's daily routine is matter-of-fact. In the first paragraph, for example, there are only two subordinate clauses. Many of the sentences are short, giving a series of vivid snapshots that are clear and reassuring. There is only a faint hint of the unusual in the phrase beginning the second paragraph – 'In a bizarre profession . . . .' The general impression is one of normality – his punctual arrival at the station of the quiet Hertfordshire town of Berkhamsted, a mere twenty-seven miles north-west of London, his waiting bicycle, his ride past the local school and the church – stable symbols of a secure and settled way of life. Finally he rides down the unpretentious King's Road to his semi-detached house, lets himself in with his Yale key and calls out to his wife . . .

THE HUMAN FACTOR

Castle was usually able to catch the six thirty-five train from Euston. This brought him to Berkhamsted punctually at seven twelve. His bicycle waited for him at the station – he had known the ticket collector for many years and he always left it in his care. Then he rode the longer way home, for the sake of exercise – across the canal bridge, past the Tudor school, into the High Street, past the grey flint parish church which contained the helmet of a crusader, then up the slope of the Chilterns towards his small semi-detached house in King's Road. He always arrived there, if he had not telephoned a warning from London, by half past seven. There was just time to say good night to the boy and have a whisky or two before dinner at eight.

In a bizarre profession anything which belongs to an everyday routine gains great value – perhaps that was one reason why, when he came back from South Africa, he chose to return to his birthplace: to the canal under the weeping willows, to the school and the ruins of a once-famous castle which had withstood a siege by Prince John of France and of which, so the story went, Chaucer had been a Clerk of Works and – who knows? – perhaps an ancestral Castle one of the artisans. It consisted now of only a few grass mounds and some yards of flint wall, facing the canal and the railway line. Beyond was a long road leading away from the town bordered with hawthorn hedges and Spanish chestnut trees until one reached at last the freedom of the Common . . . .

When Castle was a child there still remained on the Common the remnants of old trenches dug in the heavy red clay during the first

German .... It was unsafe to wander there without proper knowledge, since the old trenches had been dug several feet deep, modelled on the original trenches of the Old Contemptibles around Ypres, and a stranger risked a sudden fall and a broken leg. Children who had grown up with the knowledge of their whereabouts wandered freely, until the memory began to fade. Castle for some reason had always remembered, and sometimes on his days off from the office he took Sam by the hand and introduced him to the forgotten hiding places and the multiple dangers of the Common.

Graham Greene's vocabulary, his sentence structures and the imagery are deliberately simple and obvious, resulting in a style that is admirably suitable for its purpose. In a sense it is unremarkable, as its very purpose is to present a disarming picture of the humdrum domestic routine which is Maurice Castle's reassuring background and cover for the web of intrigue and deception that are the reality of his life. In these opening scenes, Graham Greene reveals a masterly command of the English language that will repay careful study, for his is an art that conceals art.

Suggestions for further reading

FOSTER, B.: *The Changing English Language*, Macmillan, London, 1968.

FOWLER, H. W.: *Modern English Usage*, Oxford University Press, Oxford, revised edition, 1968.

FOWLER, H. W. and F. G.: *The King's English*, Oxford University Press, Oxford, third edition, 1978.

GOWERS, E.: *The Complete Plain Words*, Penguin Books, Harmondsworth, revised edition, 1975.

HERBERT, A.: *What a Word*, Methuen, London, 1949.

ONIONS, C. T.: *Advanced English Syntax*, Kegan Paul, London, 1905.

PARTRIDGE, E.: *Usage and Abusage*, Penguin Books, Harmondsworth, revised edition, 1973.

ROGET, P.: *Thesaurus of English Words and Phrases*, Longman, London, revised edition, 1982.

SMITH, L. P.: *The English Language*, Williams & Norgate, London, 1912.

SMITH, L. P.: *Words and Idioms*, Constable, London, 1949.

SWAN, M.: *Oxford Practical English Usage*, Oxford University Press, Oxford, 1980.

TREBLE, H. A. and VALLINS, G. H.: *The ABC of English Usage*, Oxford University Press, Oxford, 1951.

VALLINS, G. H.: *Good English: How to write it*, Pan Books, London, 1951.

VALLINS, G. H.: *Better English*, Pan Books, London, 1953.

WARNER, G. T.: *On the Writing of English*, Blackie, London, 1940.

WOOD, F. T.: *Current English Usage*, Macmillan, London, 1962.

Index

The author of this Handbook

COLIN G. HEY took a double honours degree in Philosophy and English in the University of Wales and subsequently obtained an MA (Wales) in Education and an MA (ED.) in Educational Psychology from the University of Birmingham. He taught English for sixteen years in various grammar schools, and for four years in Spain. For twenty-two years he held the post of Inspector of Schools to the Birmingham Education Committee, followed by three years as Chief Inspector of English with the Ministry of Education, Khartoum, Sudan. As an Inspector in England and in the Sudan he was actively concerned with in-service teacher training in his field of English.